THE PRIVATE DON

THE PRIVATE DON

The man behind the legend of Don Bradman

CHRISTINE WALLACE

ALLEN&UNWIN

This paperback edition published in 2007
First published in 2004

Allen & Unwin
83 Alexander Street
Crows Nest NSW 2065
Australia
Phone: (61 2) 8425 0100
Fax: (61 2) 9906 2218
Email: info@allenandunwin.com
Web: www.allenandunwin.com

National Library of Australia
Cataloguing-in-Publication entry:
Wallace, Christine, 1960–
The private Don : the man behind the legend of Don Bradman.

Bibliography.
Includes index.
ISBN 978 1 74175 158 1 (pbk.).

1. Bradman, Donald Sir, 1908–2001 – Friends and associates.
2. Rivett, Rohan, 1917–1977 – Friends and associates.
3. Cricket players – Australia – Biography. I. Title.

796.358092

Edited by Jo Jarrah
Typeset by Midland Typesetters
Index by Fay Donlevy
Cover and text design by Phil Campbell
Cover image by Getty Images
Printed in Australia by McPherson's Printing Group
10 9 8 7 6 5 4 3 2 1

Contents

I *The Letters*

'I think most people, and probably that includes you, regard me as a difficult & even cantankerous soul. Really I'm not. In fact I'm rather meek, very shy etc, but I confess to an inquiring & individualistic mind with a very pugnacious streak which says that a thing is not necessarily right because others say so.'

– DON BRADMAN

Limelight is illumination of the most unreliable kind. It tricks the incurious and unquesting into the belief that what they see is all that is there. Donald Bradman, sporting great and Australian icon, is the example par excellence. Seven decades of national adoration and intense media attention burned the image of the batsman in the baggy green cap, with the slight grin and wickedly dancing eyes looking coolly up the wicket, into the Australian psyche.

But much beyond that gorgeous image, what do we know about Don Bradman? Apart from his carefully recorded cricketing career, arguably little more than a clutch of clichés and prejudices which, when tested, often find their purveyors wanting. Bradman was born in 1908 and retired from first class cricket in 1949, and most biographical treatments of his life concentrate overwhelmingly on this period. Yet he lived on for another half century. Biographical work on this part of Bradman's life is scant. The relative neglect is akin to reporting the first innings but not the second of a Test match, something untenable for an Australian of his stature. We need to know Bradman in the round, not just in the two dimensions the limelight illuminated – to know him and, because he looms so large in the Australian psyche of the twentieth century, to know ourselves better through him as a people and a nation.

Bradman himself knew a historical reassessment awaited him, that it would come after his death, and he considered it as a plus. 'In my few moments of triumph (if any) in the modest arena I have trodden, I have sought seclusion and peace – not publicity,' Bradman told his good friend Rohan Rivett in September 1971, at the age of sixty-three. 'But hate it as I might, publicity seems to be my lot. Perhaps my reward will come posthumously for I guess historians will assess whether I faithfully served mankind.'

The scant attention given to the second half of Bradman's life is especially surprising since he was a regular and voluminous letter writer. After rising to prominence and facing an onslaught of interest and admiration, not least via the postal service, he devoted a couple of hours daily to correspondence. Indeed, his diligent attention to it over the attractions of a drink in the bar with the boys during his playing days intensified the sense of singularity and separateness about him as a person.

The thousands of Bradman letters held in private hands are the stuff from which historians and biographers can and should draw on to deepen existing accounts of his life. Their range could well stun those who pursue them broadly for Bradman did not correspond just with the high and mighty but, in democratic spirit and with due modesty, with all comers. ASIO director-general Dennis Richardson tells the story of how the woman who cleaned house in Canberra for him and his family and some of their friends years ago once wrote to Bradman, and that quite a correspondence ensued. Its value to the historian and biographer lies precisely in the fact that, unlike the letters that have hitherto come to light, those letters are unlikely to dwell on bowling rates and cricket administration. Until energetic writers and scholars chase up caches of letters like this we will not know what such correspondents might have had to say to each other. Such exchanges may tell us something important. Identifying and accessing the scores of letters in ordinary correspondents' hands poses an enticing challenge to interested researchers.

The Bradman letters in the Rivett Papers held by the National Library of Australia point the way forward in the project of drawing Bradman in the round. The Library's decision in December 2003 to open the previously closed collection massively expands the amount of public information about Bradman the man, as opposed to Bradman the icon. It is likely to become the starting point for writers and scholars working on his whole life, not just its 'player' half.

The Bradman letters to Rohan Rivett begin on 5 May 1953 with a business letter sent to Rivett in his capacity as editor-in-chief of the *News*, Adelaide's now defunct afternoon daily newspaper. Bradman's last letter to the man who quickly became his close friend and sparring partner was written in September 1977. Throughout the twenty-four year correspondence Bradman lived in Adelaide at his 2 Holden Street, Kensington Park home where he resided until his death in February 2001. Except for two years based in Zurich, Switzerland, Rivett lived in Camberwell, Melbourne for the bulk of the correspondence while regularly travelling the world. The series ends with a letter from Bradman to Rohan's wife Nancy 'Nan' Rivett in October 1977 upon Rohan's sudden death. The correspondence is a jewel in the rich manuscripts collection of the National Library, and grail for Bradman devotees seeking insights into The Don.

Even more, the correspondence is a window into close friendship between two twentieth century Australian men in an era when the term 'mate' was applied indiscriminately, often obscuring more than illuminating male relationships. It sheds light on the real Bradman and tests the increasingly common wisdom about him – that he was a Tory and anti-Catholic. The letters suggest that on these two scores he has been verballed for at least half a century. Bradman did not publicly defend himself against false accusations during his lifetime. In death, the opening of these letters allows the historical record to be righted and misapprehensions corrected. For a figure so significant to the Australian national psyche and sense of self, this is a matter of immense public interest and import.

Don Bradman was born in 1908 in Cootamundra, New South Wales – halfway between Sydney and Melbourne – the youngest of George and Emily Bradman's five children. His youth in the Southern Highlands town of Bowral, where the family moved for better prospects and where Emily had family links, was famously secure and idyllic. His father had regular employment as a carpenter and the family straddled working and lower middle class status. George Bradman was an enthusiastic cricketer and cricket administrator with the local team, but the family were not cricket obsessives – nor were they, or the young Don Bradman himself, overly dazzled by his precocious interest and ability in the game including, somewhat oddly for a youth, in club administration.

Bradman famously spent hundreds of solitary hours hitting a golf ball back and forth with a stump against the concrete base of the family's galvanised iron water tank, perfecting his batsman's eye and reflexes at lightning sharp speeds. But this was also a cricket prodigy who took a couple of years off to play tennis in his teens. Nor was the cricketer he describes as his boyhood hero one of the showy greats but rather J.M. 'Johnny' Taylor, an Australian test batsman from 1920 to 1926. 'Somehow or other, his style of batting, his superb outfielding and innate modesty made a deep impression on me,' Bradman wrote in 1977 of his feelings as a thirteen year old boy. 'From the day I saw him play on the Sydney Cricket Ground in 1921, I sought to emulate his example.'

The teenage Bradman's return to the game was seamless. Bradman himself dated his serious cricket career from the beginning of summer, 1925, when at the age of seventeen he became a regular member of the Bowral cricket team, combining it at first with a continued interest in tennis. His stellar batting performances for Bowral attracted the attention of state cricket selectors and in 1926 he was invited to play for Sydney first grade club St George. The teenage Bradman, then employed by Bowral real estate agent Percy Westbrook, would travel to and from the Southern Highlands on Saturdays to play for St George. Still he did not abandon tennis. The limit of the highly supportive Westbrook for these sporting endeavours was reached when Bradman found himself chosen to play both in Country Week Tennis and Country Week Cricket, then major tournaments for talented players. 'Mr Westbrook never placed any obstacles in the way,' Bradman wrote in his memoirs, 'but on this occasion he made it clear that I could have leave to play in one Country Week, but not both. Cricket won.' He subsequently moved to Sydney, at first also employed in a new Sydney office opened by Westbrook.

A year after Bradman crystallised his commitment to cricket over tennis, he was selected to play Sheffield Shield for NSW. The following year, 1928, he reached the pinnacle: selection in the Australian team. At just twenty years old, Bradman played his first Test match, against England at the Brisbane Exhibition Ground, scoring an inauspicious 18 and 1. But it was all up and up from there. At the end of his playing days Bradman's Test batting average of 99.94 was almost twice as good as the next most successful batsmen in the game, and still is.

Springbok quick A.J. Bell recorded his and his team-mates' first impressions of Bradman, about whom they had already heard much, three years later at the outset of their 1931–32 tour of Australia. They were surprised to see on first meeting 'a tiny fellow in a neat grey suit', a good conversationalist with probing eyes, out to learn all he could, and giving the impression of being an astute businessman.

Bowling to Bradman turned out to be a heartbreaking experience according to Bell who, observing the risks the Australian took at the crease, said he never seemed to pay the price his temerity merited. Bradman's stamina at the wicket astonished the Springboks, as did the fact that he barely seemed to perspire: 'Our bowlers used to get through three of our shirts a day, but Don comes out in an immaculate silk shirt at noon and at six o'clock it is still an immaculate silk shirt.'

Hundreds of thousands of words have been written about Bradman's cricket prowess. The style, the statistics, the mental fortitude and powers of concentration have all been explored exhaustively. However, the inner Bradman remained an enigma, not least to some of his team-mates who never came to grips with his disinclination to carry on like 'one of the boys'. What is more, his post-cricket playing days far exceeded his playing ones, a half century during which his importance to Australia and Australians grew, rather than diminished. Bradman became even more delphic after he retired from first class cricket in 1949 than he had been before. Living in the relative backwater of Adelaide, where he moved in 1934 to develop a new career as a stockbroker in parallel to cricket, made this easier to achieve than it might have had he remained in Sydney. With him went his wife of two years, Jessie (nee Menzies), his sweetheart from Bowral days. In 1936 they had a son who died shortly after birth. Son John followed in 1939 and daughter Shirley was born in 1941. Both children suffered significant health challenges – John with childhood polio, from which he staged a full recovery, and depression in early adulthood, and Shirley with an intellectual disability which developed in early childhood. Don and Jessie's marriage was strong, lasting sixty-five years before Jessie's death in 1997. It thrived despite the family health difficulties, with Bradman's own repeated bouts of painful fibrositis and, later in life, Jessie's heart disease, adding to their worries about the children. Bradman was devoted to Jessie, John and Shirley. He seemed to take special delight in Shirley whose positive attitude, irrespective of her disability, mirrored his own. His care and concern for John took a long time to wear thin in the face of his son's diffidence about the future, and the two reconciled later in life. Bradman's earnings as a stockbroker and company director saw him amply fulfil the then traditional role of family provider. Bradman died in 2001, ninety-two years old, still living in the Kensington Park home in which he and Jessie had raised their family.

The *Age*'s Graham Perkin, interviewing him in 1959,

observed that Bradman had been an 'imponderable personality' throughout his playing days – that no-one knew what he was really like, though many thought they did. Like A.J. Bell all those years before, Perkin found Bradman, then aged fifty-one, in the lounge of his Kensington Park home an 'ordinary, small man in a grey suit'. But as Bradman sat and sipped a cup of tea, another impression came through strongly: that if he had put on flannels and pads and walked out to the wicket that day, 'he would surely get a fast hundred'.

More than a decade later, Jeff Thomson told journalist Michael Parkinson about an incident in the 1970s where Bradman, by then well into his sixties, was approached at a cricket field social function by two young players on the cusp of state selection who asked whether they might bowl to him. Bradman pointed out that he hadn't played for thirty years, but picked up a bat and readied for a ball. 'At first the young men bowled respectfully at him, aware both of his age and the fact that he had neither pads nor gloves,' Parkinson recounts Thomson telling him. 'But when Bradman started playing shots, they quickened up and eventually were bowling flat out. According to Thomson, the quicker they bowled, the harder Bradman smote them to the boundary.' He was a sporting titan – young, middle-aged, old. But beyond that, who was he, really?

Before and after his retirement from first class cricket, Bradman kept his own counsel about his life and the things that mattered to him. This was his nature: he was no blow-hard, no grandstander. The innate modesty that had made Johnny Taylor such an appealing role model to him as a thirteen year old test cricket spectator was the keynote of his own adult years, no matter how extraordinary his sporting achievements became. Silence on personal matters and issues of national controversy was one facet of it, maintained until the end.

This had three main consequences. Firstly, it had a kind of 'Japanese emperor' effect. The more silent Bradman was, the more the legend grew: a kind of secular deification was fuelled. This was without doubt unintentional and perversely intensified public interest in him – something which life tucked away in sleepy Adelaide was at least partly designed to avoid.

It made him something of a *tabula rasa* onto which enemies could paint and project criticisms and falsehoods effectively without challenge, the principal charge being that he was anti-Catholic. 'His greatest critics, Jack Fingleton and Bill O'Reilly who both played under his captaincy, let their bias, jealousy and animosity rise to the surface in their writings,' as former test cricket colleague and fellow Australian selector Sam Loxton has observed. Bradman's reticence gave critics like these open slather. The transaction costs of undermining Bradman's reputation behind the scenes and in public were close to zero because he would not come out and defend himself. Since there was no price to be paid for doing so, the critics could keep white-anting away.

It made it easier for people to appropriate the Bradman legend for their own purposes. At the benign end of the spectrum is the pervasive myth of the boy from the bush emerging to slay all before him with untutored sporting genius, reinforcing a particular Australian male archetype still extremely popular today. Cricket buff and writer Rodney Cavalier has made a major contribution to correcting this myth, arguing that there was probably no other player in the history of Australian cricket who had the odds so heavily stacked in their favour. Bradman's family were cricket friendly, connected and capable: there was cricket talent on both sides of the family, and both George and Emily would bowl to their youngest son in the backyard. Bowral was a big cricket town and part of a strong rural competition. He grew up in a loving family in a healthy environment. As Cavalier concludes: 'It is hard to perceive what element of the Don's magnificent triumph was against the odds . . .'

At the less benign end of the spectrum are the subtle – and not so subtle – efforts to make Bradman a poster boy for Tory politics and values. Academic Brett Hutchins has opened up territory here which merits pursuit, drawing attention to the use of cricket and its heroes, notably Bradman, by Liberal Prime Minister John Howard in the political ruse of building appeal through vicarious association. Howard has given this old game new legs. 'His lauding of the Don and his friendship with [former Australian captain] Mark Taylor follows Menzies' example,' Hutchins points out.

While not uniformly successful, Hutchins' attempt to open up one of Australia's core archetypes – the Bradman legend – for critical analysis deserves real credit. This is especially so given the powerful, well-connected and generously funded apparatus which attempts to manage the myth through continuing close control of artefacts and images of Bradman the man. Given The Don's central role in Australians' sense of national identity – at least for Australian men – that is a project that could easily spill over into censorship of the national identity debate itself. For the health of the polity, that would not be a good thing.

It is important to separate Bradman himself from the efforts of others to appropriate his mythic power for their own purposes. Just as Bradman did not publicly respond to slurs from those with animus towards him, nor did he neutralise others' attempts to appropriate him politically. And just as Bradman's silence in response to attacks on his reputation did not signify confirmation of the slurs against him, nor did silence in response to attempted political appropriation signify assent to such manoeuvres or his political identification with those forces.

How can this be asserted? Until the National Library's recent opening of the previously closed correspondence between Bradman and Rohan Rivett it could not be, with confidence. Nancy Rivett's donation of the letters to the Library, and the Library's decision to open them to public scrutiny, is a major contribution to knowledge about Bradman, his life, his views, and therefore to his relationship with Australia and Australia's relationship with him.

This is the first time any and every Australian can directly engage with the man underpinning the mythic figure, and move beyond the *tabula rasa* which has had the unintended consequences outlined earlier. For in the intimate twenty-four year exchange of letters between these two friends, there was no need for diplomacy or artfulness, and no place for deceit.

Less well known than Bradman, obviously, outside newspaper circles, was Rohan Rivett. Rivett's name survives in contemporary history mainly because of his relationship with media mogul Rupert Murdoch. While still at Oxford Rupert Murdoch inherited the *News*, of which Rivett was the dynamic editor-in-chief. A seasoned journalist fourteen years older than the young Murdoch, Rivett had been a favourite of Rupert's father, Sir Keith Murdoch, at the *Herald* in Melbourne. Sir Keith posted Rivett to London in 1948 and from there appointed him editor-in-chief of the *News* in 1951. Rivett was just thirty-four years old. The *News* was Sir Keith's main legacy to Rupert who, on that modest foundation, spent half a century building one of the biggest media conglomerates in the world.

Rivett's arrival at the *News* gave the old-fashioned tabloid a jolt. As one of Sir Keith's favourites, 'he had a foothold on Olympus' recalls distinguished journalist and editor David Bowman, then a young cadet. 'Tall, erect, he swept through the corridors as if he owned them, spoke to people, moved in an aura of youthful energy and purpose. There was an eager note in his voice and he smiled easily. He had a natural air of command and, as one soon learned, acted decisively. Not an instant to waste; Rivett the urgent journalist marched into the office lavatory bearing a portable wireless tuned to the news so as not to miss anything.'

When Rupert arrived in Adelaide in September 1953, the relationship with the new young master was at the outset warm and collegiate. Rupert was no stranger. Rupert and his father had holidayed in Europe with the Rivetts, and Rupert used to visit them from Oxford for some home cooking during Rohan's London posting. In Adelaide he worked hard with Rohan by day and socialised with him and Nancy after hours as well. Rupert played rough-house games with the Rivett boys, David and Keith, the latter named after Rupert's father, but even in them Rupert always had to win, according to family legend. The Rivetts' daughter Rhyll recalls Rupert taking her and her brothers for spins in his flash car around the sedate streets of the South Australian capital. He was fun, but fast and somewhat dangerous fun to the younger Rivetts.

Adelaide was a small city of less than half a million people when Rupert Murdoch moved there. The presence of an educated, cosmopolitan figure like Rivett, who knew the good life and lived it even in that arch conservative Adelaide epoch, would have been something of a saviour for the twenty-two year old proprietor. Nancy Rivett, a successful Melbourne actress at the time of her marriage to Rivett and a woman of immense style and charm, was another magnet. Murdoch biographer William Shawcross reports that Murdoch's family in Melbourne feared for his social safety in 1950s Adelaide, which they considered a 'wilderness'.

Rivett's secretary at the *News*, Joy Saunders, took care of Murdoch too, until he could engage his own secretary. 'While taking dictation from Rupert one day,' she recounted, 'we were interrupted by a phone call and, after he'd hung up, Rupert said: "These Adelaide matrons – all after me for their daughters"!!!' There may have been some comfort that a favourite of Sir Keith's was around to help Rupert learn the ropes and survive Adelaide's small town mores. But sentimentality did not play a decisive role in the newcomer's business decisions. As former colleague and fellow favourite of Murdoch senior Keith Dunstan put it: 'Being a Murdoch man did one no good after Sir Keith died.'

The relationship gradually eroded, with the denouement in 1960 when Murdoch, after moving to Sydney to oversee his new tabloid, the *Daily Mirror*, famously sacked Rivett. Like the Bradman letters, Murdoch's letter of dismissal also forms part of the National Library's Rivett Papers. After 'much long and tortuous consideration', Murdoch wrote, he had reached the 'unhappy conclusion' that Rivett had to step down as editor-in-chief of the *News*. Rivett was unlikely to agree with his reasons 'which are many', so it was better not to outline them at that time, Murdoch wrote. 'Nothing would make me happier than for you to continue with the organisation as a star writer', he continued, but should Rivett not want to do so he would be compensated with a lump sum equivalent to eighteen months' salary. Murdoch told his old family friend and mentor that it had taken him days to work up to writing the letter, and he appended a handwritten note to the dismissal in which he declared he had never 'loathed' writing any letter more: 'In coming to this decision to "close your innings" as editor of the *News* I have not lost sight of all your achievements – and our long personal friendship makes the whole thing impossibly hard.'

Dame Elisabeth Murdoch later sent a handwritten note from her home, Cruden Farm, expressing concern for Rohan over the break – and for Rupert who, like her she said, felt 'wretchedness' over the move. That the two had some good years together in Adelaide was as Sir Keith would have wanted, and it had been a great comfort to her as well, 'but realising that you and Rupert are both rather unique characters with such different temperaments it has been rather remarkable that you've managed to go along together so well'. Dame Elisabeth's wishes for the relationship between the two families to remain close could not have been more warmly expressed as she closed sending love to both him and 'Nan', asking them to visit and stay in touch.

A letter from Murdoch in response to an inquiry from Rohan's daughter Rhyll Rivett thirty-six years after the dismissal sheds further light on it. Rohan was a remarkable but polarising figure as portrayed by Rupert Murdoch. He singled out Rohan's undeniable leadership qualities, his warmth, charm and attractive personality, his idealism, intolerance for injustice and instinct to fight for the underdog as positive qualities. He was a strong, inspiring speaker who used to gather the journalists and subs around him to pronounce on any number of topics, Murdoch recounted.

On the other hand, Rohan's own writings were polarising according to Murdoch – people either loved his line or hated it – and he polarised the staff of the *News*, too. Some staff idolised him, others thought his modus operandi too politically charged, not that he seemed to have any particular party political allegiance, Murdoch acknowledged.

The Rupert Max Stuart case was the turning point. Stuart was an Aboriginal sentenced to death in South Australia after being convicted of the murder of Mary Olive Hattam at Ceduna in 1958. The police investigation was wanting and Rivett believed Stuart had been wrongfully convicted. Rivett ran a trenchant campaign against the Playford Government in 1959 over the issue. This eventually yielded a royal commission, the commutation of Stuart's sentence to life imprisonment, and multiple charges against Rivett for seditious libel. The charges, perceived as political persecution of Rivett by the government which he had so relentlessly pursued, ultimately failed, but he faced the prospect of a significant prison term had they succeeded.

Murdoch signalled in his letter to Rhyll Rivett that Rohan's campaign over Rupert Max Stuart's conviction was one manifestation of something he saw as a more fundamental problem. Rohan believed Stuart had been wrongly convicted but, according to Murdoch, most readers of the *News* did not. More generally Murdoch believed that Rivett's bold and highly controversial approach was beginning to hurt the paper, turning readers against it. The circulation of the *News* was higher when Rohan departed in 1960 than it had been on his arrival in 1951, but Murdoch was the owner and that was that.

In what would become time-honoured News Limited practice Rohan, like the string of slain editors to come, was offered a well-paid senior writer's job. He declined and left Adelaide for Zurich to take up a position as director of the International Press Institute (IPI). Murdoch signed off his 1996 recollections to Rhyll 'sincerely', and sent the family his best wishes. And just like most letters to Rohan, Murdoch's letter to Rhyll singles out 'Nan' for especially warm wishes – in Murdoch's case, with an exclamation mark.

The difference between Rivett and many others who later came to feel Murdoch's steel was Rivett's considerable standing and accomplishment independent of his career in journalism. Born in 1917 Rohan was the tall, golden-haired son of knighted scientist and academic David Rivett, the founder of the CSIRO's forerunner, the Council for Scientific and Industrial Research, and Stella Deakin, daughter of noted early twentieth century prime minister Alfred Deakin. Rohan carried many of his grandfather Deakin's small 'l' liberal values forward throughout his long journalistic career, coming to the media via Wesley College, Melbourne University, Oxford and the AIF. The die was cast even before he left school. At thirteen, visiting England with his father, Rohan wrote a long account of the 1930 Ashes series where he thrilled to the young Donald Bradman's batting.

During World War II, after being seconded by the AIF to work on radio news bulletins and commentaries in Melbourne, he resigned to volunteer for work in Singapore with the Malaya Broadcasting Corporation. Singapore's fall to advancing Japanese forces was announced to the world by Rivett in 1942 via radio broadcast. He escaped the island by sea but was captured a few weeks later and despatched to the hellish Thai–Burma Railway. His account of that three year imprisonment, *Behind Bamboo*, was a post-war best-seller.

In the words of former secretary Delme Forbes, Rivett was 'Brainy, Bright, Unpredictable, Erratic, a One-Off': the capital letters were no mistake. Forbes responded to an advertisement in the *Times* for a position with the International Press Institute in Zurich in the early 1960s. Rivett rang at 7.30 am one day calling her to an interview at the Tavistock Hotel in London that evening. Rather than asking the standard interview questions, Rohan gave a 'vivid and exciting description' of the IPI and his vision for it over a pot of tea in the Tavistock's lounge. At a follow-up interview the next day he argued passionately about press freedom, confided he hated living in Zurich and asked her to bring a suit from his London tailor with her when she came to Switzerland. Two days later a formal letter arrived, handwritten in red ink, offering Forbes the job.

'Working with him was never dull – the staff of that time would all agree there was an air of excitement,' Forbes recalled. 'I learned that in some areas he was curiously sensitive – a colleague who failed to personally sign an official communication could plunge him into gloom, a facetious remark over some minor matter could earn you a severe blasting.' But Rivett built Forbes' confidence and convinced her she was efficient and could tackle any challenge she faced: 'His faith stood me in good stead over the years.'

Again, however, Rivett's sweeping manoeuvres in line with his own passionate agenda at the IPI, which was dominated by American and European interests, caused some strong reactions. 'He was a very dynamic person and he introduced many changes in IPI and he was deeply interested in the editorial development of the undeveloped countries, particularly the Far Eastern countries,' recalls K.M. Mathew of Indian newspaper *Malayala Manorama*. 'He concentrated mainly on places like India and Africa and he had to face [a] lot of problems from the West. His efforts were not appreciated by many others in the organization and he resigned in disgust.'

Rivett's passion for the less developed world was genuine, longstanding and partly inherited. For forty years his much loved aunt, Eleanor Rivett, worked in India as a teacher and principal in girls' schools. Her brother, Rohan's father David, toured India extensively with her on the way to take up his 1907 Rhodes Scholarship at Oxford.

But it was Rohan's insight into the conditions of the poor in Asia during his experience as a Japanese POW that was the intensely personal propellant for his Asian passion according to his widow Nancy: 'He wrote about our relationship with Asia light years before our present day politicians.' Nan Rivett points to an article on the Colombo Conference in 1950 as evidence of Rohan's prescience. 'For those of us who live in Australasia, genuine mutual confidence and really friendly relations with our neighbours of southern Asia and the islands between are at least as important as friendship with her western European neighbours is for Britain today,' Rohan wrote. 'For to the people of Java, Sumatra, Malaya, Siam, China and India we are now "the folk next door". We can no longer afford to ignore them, nor they us, if each of us is to assure the most favourable climate for our own national development and safety.'

In his unpublished 1996 recollections to Rhyll Rivett, Rupert Murdoch singled out the increased emphasis on international events as Rivett's most significant contribution to the *News*. He tactfully failed to mention the incident that caused even Rivett's biggest supporters to feel he may have taken the international bent a little too far: the front page splash on the death of British Labour politician Aneurin Bevan in 1960. The whole of page one was given over to Bevan's death as well as considerable space inside the paper. 'Probably Mr. Bevan was not held in high esteem by the readership as he was by Rohan,' recalled *News* journalist John Miles. 'Perhaps some had never heard of him. But as G.K. Chesterton wrote, journalism is about announcing Lord Jones is dead to people who never knew Lord Jones had been alive.'

Journalist Keith Dunstan was another who benefited from Rivett's confidence-building style. In 1946 Dunstan was a first year cadet at the *Herald* in Melbourne, fresh out of the air force. Rivett was a senior feature writer on the paper, having accepted an offer from Sir Keith Murdoch to come over from the *Argus*. One of Rivett's side duties was supervision of cadets writing sport on Saturdays. Dunstan had to cover VFL football – something about which he knew little – and was called in by the chief football writer, Alf Brown, on Monday mornings to respond to complaints about the best players list in his stories.

'Just when I thought I was about to be fired there was a note from Rohan,' Dunstan said. 'He complimented me on my report of a match between Melbourne and Richmond. He said it was different to all the other reports.' Rohan told Dunstan: 'I particularly liked the line when you wrote that Geelong players so lacked in teamwork one would have thought they were waiting to be introduced to each other.' Recalls Dunstan: 'That gave me heart to continue.'

Dunstan was, however, interested in cricket and covered test matches for the *Sun-Pictorial* in the early 1960s. Rivett he remembers as fanatical about cricket, and with a prodigious memory – 'almost a walking Wisden' who could sprout Bradman's scores in specific innings, Bill O'Reilly's bowling averages, Ponsford's best innings at the Melbourne Cricket Ground (MCG) and the like.

Dunstan was a member of the Melbourne Cricket Club (MCC) and enjoyed its facilities, but on big occasions would visit the MCG's raffish Bay 13 on the lookout for column colour. 'Always I found Rohan there,' Dunstan recalled. 'He would be in the same place, standing, not sitting, under the eaves behind the last row of seats on ground level. I asked him why he did this. He said he wasn't even slightly interested in the members. He went to Bay 13 because he could get right behind the bowler's arm. Oh yes, Bay 13 was pretty rambunctious, but it was here that you found the action and it was here you found the true cricket enthusiasts. What stamina! He would just stand there for hour after hour. I still wondered why he didn't look for a seat.'

Rivett had been a major favourite of Sir Keith Murdoch, and Keith Dunstan on his own account was another, more minor, one. As such they used to swap notes on the progress of the master's son. 'Here was the young radical just out of Oxford,' Dunstan recounted Rivett saying in later years of Rupert's arrival at the *News*. 'The metamorphosis of the young left winger, in the space of just four weeks, to a right wing, hungry, self-seeking conservative was the most remarkable thing he ever witnessed. He didn't realise that a grub could turn into a moth so quickly.'

The extent to which Rivett's recollection was coloured by his sacking is hard to gauge. Some facts, however, stand out. With nine years at the top of the *News* Rivett was, by Australian standards, a fairly long-serving editor. While Murdoch undoubtedly encroached over time, Rivett is perceived to have had a pretty free hand with the paper, which was progressive, internationalist and crusading under his hand – and Rupert Murdoch was there for seven of the nine years Rivett was in charge. Rivett's departure from the *News* has always been characterised as a sacking but in fact he resigned after declining a senior writer's position on the paper – something which many former News Limited editors have since instead accepted, sometimes with great success. Ex-editors currently in high profile positions with News Limited papers in Australia include Paul Kelly, the *Australian*'s 'editor-at-large', right-wing *Daily Telegraph* columnist Piers Akerman, and Frank Devine, who has a regular column in the *Australian*. The practice spread to Fairfax where former editor-in-chief of the *Age*, Greg Hywood, for example, continues as a columnist with the paper after dismissal from the top job.

Perhaps the most unfortunate aspect of the episode was the manner in which Murdoch dispensed with Rivett's services as editor. Had it been done face-to-face and with a stronger appeal for Rivett to stay on as a senior writer – if not at the *News* then as a columnist, perhaps, on Murdoch's newly acquired *Daily Mirror* – News Limited would not have lost one of the big if mercurial talents of post-war Australian journalism. Nor would Murdoch have cruelled what was, up to that point, one of the significant relationships in his still young life. But as Murdoch biographer William Shawcross points out, relationship management was something Sir Keith Murdoch had identified as one of young Rupert's shortcomings. Shawcross cites Sir Keith in a letter to Rivett in 1952 saying that Rupert 'must learn that all human relationships, even those with his family, have always to be kept in repair; and are infinitely worth a lot of trouble and study . . .'

Reading between the lines of views from some staff of the *News* gives a hint, perhaps, of what Murdoch described as the situation in his 1996 recollections to Rhyll Rivett of Rohan's reign. '. . . I don't feel I want to go back over the Rivett years in Adelaide,' wrote Murray James to Rhyll. 'I will always remember your father as an idealist with an obsessive drive to make the world a better place in which to live. No person in my experience, did more for the working journalist than your father. I had great admiration for Nan.'

News journalist John Miles suggested that Adelaide and the paper were the wrong scale for a Rohan Rivett. 'Rohan was a big man in every sense,' Miles recalled. 'Perhaps it was his stature that caused his downfall, if it could be called that. Perhaps he was too big, too big for Adelaide, too big for the *News* and too big for some people.' Miles found him a friendly, considerate, encouraging editor but conceded some may have found him intimidating: 'He strode strongly about the office, he smoked cigars like a tycoon, but he never bullied.'

Miles said that Rivett raised the *News* to an unprecedented, and never repeated, standard. 'In doing so, he trod on toes,' he said. 'He once gathered the editorial staff together in the reporters' room for one of his "fireside chats". He told us that he thought "the Establishment" in Adelaide was too powerful and that the *News* was, to put it mildly, not on their side.' The impact of this attitude in the hidebound Adelaide of the 1950s, let alone in the mind of the editor of one of the isolated city's two daily newspapers, is mind-boggling. The *News* was no Labor stooge according to Miles, but did distinguish itself from the *Advertiser* 'slavishly supporting Tom Playford and his regime'. Playford had a hand in Rivett's downfall, Miles believed, but the end game was only part of the story. 'It was widely thought in Adelaide that Rohan was sacked over his handling of the Rupert Stuart murder case,' Miles said. 'But it was much more complicated than that. Perhaps he was just too big a man.'

Some of Rivett's gestures were small but powerfully positive in their impact. Rita Dunstan wrote a series of stories for the paper about the plight of poor pensioners. Rivett suggested at a story conference that the *News* should launch a charity drive for the aged poor. The paper launched the 'Pounds for Pensioners' campaign and raised ten thousand pounds in the run-up to Christmas one year, with considerable positive glow for the *News*. 'Often at social functions friends would produce their cheque books (un-asked) and write a donation for the fund,' recalled Dunstan. It was, she said, wholly and solely Rivett's idea.

Journalism was a calling, he believed: it mattered, and should be put to enlightened use, David Bowman recalled of his charismatic editor's views. 'You could be proud to write for his newspaper,' Bowman said. 'He moved confidently among the powerful and was not afraid.' But Bowman, a huge admirer, nevertheless said he glimpsed Rivett 'inflated' during the height of the Stuart controversy, taking the reporting a step beyond that merited on the facts. He recalled returning to the *News* from the Royal Commission, which he had been assigned to cover, on the day it broke up following a walkout by Stuart's counsel: 'The [newspaper's] posters were already on display and I felt a chill as I read them. This wasn't how I had seen things.' Rivett was rejoicing in the office at the turn of events, and in the face of his boss's euphoria Bowman felt unable to mount the argument that the paper's line had gone too far on a matter far too grave.

Bowman remained a friend and admirer: even great editors sometimes fall short, he said. When Murdoch's letter of dismissal finally arrived it was shattering, according to Bowman: 'Constantinople had fallen, Christendom lay open to the unbelievers. The greatest tribute to Rivett was the horror that Murdoch caused among journalists, the wild hopes that lived on that Rivett would start a paper on his own, and the exodus that began as reality sank in.' Soon the *News* reverted to its pre-Rivett torpor. Now it no longer exists at all. There is an interesting thesis to be explored about the extent to which this single episode determined the attitude of Australian journalists to Rupert Murdoch as a media proprietor so early in his career, and how different things might have been. But that is another story.

The opening letter of the correspondence in May 1953 is Bradman's reply to Rivett's invitation to cover that year's Ashes series in England for the *News*, which Bradman was also to cover for the English *Daily Mail*. The commissioning of the 1953 Test coverage was the genesis of a close friendship between the two men. As business correspondence, and addressed to 'Rohan Rivett Esq.', the first Bradman letter in the Rivett Papers was by necessity formal in style and salutation. The next letter in the series some seven weeks later in June, sent by Bradman from Northcliffe House in London concerning his coverage of the Tests, was noticeably, though only marginally, less formal. 'Dear Mr Rivett' has been replaced by 'Dear Rohan', and the sign-off has relaxed somewhat into: 'With very kind regards, Yours sincerely, Don Bradman.' However, there is already an air of Bradman coming directly to grips with both the newspaper editor and the man as he details at length the logistics of his test coverage, and defends his particular approach and style.

The pace of familiarity picks up again in the following month, July. The addressee is still 'Rohan Rivett Esq.', but the sign-off is now: 'With very kindest regards to your wife and self, Yours sincerely, Don.' Later the same month this segued into 'Warmest regards . . .' Then follows an almost nine-year gap in the letters during which, the later correspondence shows, Bradman and Rivett became the closest of friends. The exchanges are frequent; scarce opportunities to meet in person, especially together with Bradman's wife Jessie and Nan Rivett, were carefully pinned down. The letters in both directions are signed off with love for the other's family, in the warmest terms.

Why did Bradman and Rivett, nine years his junior, fall into a lockstep of intimate decades-long friendship? The series consists almost entirely of Bradman's letters to Rivett. Only a few in the other direction are in the collection. However, Bradman's tendency to respond to Rivett's letters point by point generally gives a clear idea of their content.

The two men shared a deep love of cricket. Bradman was the cricketer without peer, here and abroad – a god of the game. The best-ever player in the best-loved sport in the most sports-loving nation in the world, his standing was stratospheric, his knowledge unparalleled, yet in public, his private persona was elusive to a point close on mute. Rivett was a cricket aficionado from childhood with a deep passion for and knowledge of the mythic game and strong opinions about it. Those intensely held opinions ranged across cricket practices and policy including the makeup of test teams, the pace at which the modern game was played, and its promotion to young people. As a seasoned and respected journalist and editor, Rivett was used to asserting his opinions categorically and enjoying space on the public stage – in editorials, opinion pieces and the like – to advance them.

These contending forces led to some colossal conflicts over the great game in the privacy of the correspondence. Their argument in the 1960s about bowling rates, for example, brought out the didact in Bradman. 'All your investigation as to scoring rates and bowling rates amuses me because I am Australia's No.1 authority thereon,' Bradman wrote his friend. Bradman told Rivett batsmen should not be blamed for scoring slowly when they did not receive the same number of balls in a given time. And Bradman didn't hold back when determined to ram home a point of analysis: 'I have taken out the scoring rate per 100 balls bowled for every test series this century & I don't think anyone else in the world has done that.'

Cricket is the cord that runs through the correspondence, tying the Bradman–Rivett dialogue together. Rivett was the opinionated angel who went where others more circumspect – or on less intimate terms with The Don – would fear to tread on cricket matters. Bradman, in turn, seemed to enjoy Rivett's complete refusal to be awed or intimidated by him, even on the turf of his special subject.

But there is another cord entwined with that of cricket that glued these men together: family. Don and Jessie Bradman and Rohan and Nan Rivett were a tight foursome. The pressure valve the correspondence constituted for what was an extraordinarily difficult Bradman family life cannot be underestimated. Rivett was the trusted repository for Bradman's most profound confidences about those difficulties. The shared concern for the families on both sides recurs throughout the correspondence, deeply felt. Bradman's love and commitment to his family, especially the much loved Jessie, beats like a strong heart through the letters, even when – perhaps especially when – Bradman is at his most tired and care-worn. His great affection for Nan Rivett comes through more and more clearly and playfully as the years go by.

The insatiable claims by outsiders on the time and nervous energy of the two men also constituted a common burden. This may be obvious in relation to Bradman, who was besieged for decades by the voracious attention of the media, fans, charities, and social and sporting organisations. But in its own way it was also true of Rivett. Adelaide was a small yet intense provincial place when they got to know each other in the 1950s. As editor-in-chief of the *News*, Rivett was a very big wheel in a very small city. That this was its own significant pressure even after Rivett had left Adelaide, and that the Bradmans were seen by the Rivetts as precious exceptions to it, comes through clearly in one of the few letters in the series from Rohan to Don.

'We are coming in from Manila arriving Adelaide airport 2 pm on Friday, September 7,' Rivett wrote from the Montreaux Palace Hotel in Switzerland in early July 1962. 'Please keep this to yourself and Jessie for I don't want to be inundated with people wanting me to have a drink with them, wanting a job, wanting to sell me something or just wanting to ring us up on the phone. We have to fly to Melbourne at 2 pm on Wednesday, September 12, so will have just five days in Adelaide. You pick your night, nominate it and I'll keep it free no matter what.'

Bradman's thinking and writing as expressed in the letters was extremely precise. The correspondence has the occasional crossed wire and short, sharp conflict which Bradman invariably attributed to errors on Rivett's part. These are, variously, that Rivett had missed the clearly stated point made in the preceding letter from Bradman, that he wrongly extrapolated from matters raised by Bradman; or that Rivett had his facts wrong. Such cases are the exception rather than the rule, however, and Rivett in any case had occasional cause himself to upbraid Bradman. The main example is Rivett's long, controlled but nuclear-strength rebuttal of Bradman's passing jibe to the effect that Rivett's political views and affluent lifestyle were at odds. Overwhelmingly, though, warmth and good humour permeate the letters. Bradman's wit was wry and sharp, though only occasionally did he tell an actual joke. He was not beyond poking fun at himself: 'Girth is increasing – wisdom doubtful,' he quipped as the years rolled on.

The book is organised with the topics of specialist interest – Bradman's calls as an investment analyst and his views on cricket – coming first, followed by matters of general interest. The final chapter seeks to draw the threads together in a review and critique of the letters in terms of Bradman's significance to, and impact on, Australian life and culture. Readers will for the first time be able to draw their own conclusions about the common wisdom concerning Bradman. Some may be surprised.

2 *Cricket*

'Cricket will ebb & flow – aspects of the game must change – but I cannot go along with the all too prevalent "knocking" of modern cricket (that does nothing to uplift it). The subject is too complex . . . But we'll go on loving the game & we'll get our pleasant surprises . . .'

— Don Bradman

Australia had held the Ashes for a generation when Don Bradman went to England to cover the 1953 Ashes series for the *News* and *Daily Mail*. The series was to have an unexpectedly interesting result. Bradman looked every bit the sharp sports reporter, on the spot at Nottingham's Trent Bridge ground talking to muscular England captain Len Hutton before the First Test. Rain-affected, the match was drawn but not before some skilful play was enjoyed. English fast-medium bowler Alec Bedser starred (7/55 and 7/44) but a doughty century by Australian captain Lindsay Hassett kept Australian spirits up. It was the Second Test that got Bradman's pulse rate up.

The 1953 Lord's Test match was a 'smasher', Bradman wrote home to Rivett, and his reasoning encapsulates his attitude to play overall. The cricket was less skilful than that at the First Test in Nottingham, 'but the drama of it made up for anything else'. Bradman loved exciting cricket. Criticisms of dull play and defensive mindsets, and the harm they caused the game, were a constant theme in the correspondence with Rivett. Australia was poised to win, with England on 73 for 4 wickets and five hours' play still to go. But England gutsed it out. English batsmen Willie Watson and Trevor Bailey withstood a vigorous Australian attack, lasting five and four hours respectively at the crease before their wickets fell, and were instrumental in holding the match to a draw.

In contrast the Manchester Test was, apart from a couple of brief moments, 'virtually a hopeless proposition from the first ball', and the match was another draw. Cricket matches can just go that way and the weather may have played a part, he told Rivett, in what appeared to be a little slippage in the Australians' game. While it was now mid-summer in England, cold weather and showers overwhelmed the occasional fine breaks. Late English summer always held the most promise, according to Bradman, who predicted an Australian revival in August. England had done well to hold Australia, despite three lost tosses, he thought. But England captain Hutton faced an awkward situation since if England lost one of the next two Tests they could not wrench the Ashes off Australia given that a tied series would result in the incumbent holding on to the urn. 'If England can win confronted by that situation, they will indeed have done a fine job,' he told Rohan.

The Fourth Test at Headingley at the end of July saw another draw, with time again being lost through rain. Australia was frustrated by England's passive aggressive tactics: slow batting and negative field placements. Cricket historian Chris Harte reports that someone with a perverse sense of humour had seated Bradman next to former England captain and bodyline villain Douglas Jardine in the Headingley press box.

When the deciding Fifth Test began at The Oval in mid-August, Australian captain Lindsay Hassett won the toss for the fifth match in a row and went in to bat. It was downhill from there. England won by 8 wickets, and retrieved the Ashes lost in the Fifth Test at the same ground nineteen years earlier to Bill Woodfull's touring Australians – a match in which Bradman (244 and 77) and Bill Ponsford, in his last Test, together put on 451 for the second wicket – a record which stood for sixty-three years.

Bradman returned to Adelaide, took off his journalist's hat, returned to his stock and share analysis and consolidated his and Jessie's nascent friendship with the Rivetts. But as an administrator and selector he was very much preoccupied with doing something to lift Australian cricket which had visibly slipped into the doldrums.

When he commissioned Bradman's coverage of the 1953 Ashes tour, Rivett was just two years into his nine year editorship of the *News*. The correspondence did not resume until early 1962, after Rivett took up his post as director of the International Press Institute in Zurich and personal meetings became infrequent. The cricket dialogue that ensued over the next fifteen years was very much concerned with how to boost the game in the face of perceived decline. On Bradman's part, too, it was about keeping comparisons with the past rooted in empirical data rather than romantic memories, and heading off Rivett's occasional tendency to fall into the 'they were giants in those days' syndrome.

'Bright cricket' – alive, entertaining and, within the rules, played to win – was Bradman's touchstone. Pakistan had announced it intended to play bright cricket in England, Bradman told Rivett in April 1962. But used to being disappointed in such matters he added it would be astonishing if the intention was actually achieved. The MCC had also agreed on a "throwing" truce' for the tour, Bradman confided, about which he again was dubious, telling Rivett to watch for fireworks over the extremely sensitive bowling action issue in the First Test between the two countries. Not that Bradman's scepticism – or brutal realism, perhaps – was reserved for Pakistan's England tour. In the same letter he said that he and MCC chairman of selectors Dick Robbins had agreed on bright cricket in the next Ashes tour by England, scheduled for the summer of 1962–63. 'We will see,' Bradman closed.

Rivett, as it turned out, was in London in June for one of the Pakistan matches. 'We saw a great Saturday at Lords (when the Pakistan captain and No. 8 made centuries) from the vantage point of the clock tower box and at least six dry martinis,' Rivett wrote. 'This is much the best way to watch Pakistan playing cricket. It does not allow you to give the cricket any more importance than the English bowlers and fieldsmen give it, which is not very much at all.' It was doubtful whether Pakistan would beat even St Kilda, Melbourne or Fitzroy District firsts, Rivett went on. 'The fielding has to be seen to be believed and their batting is more unpredictable than the Zurich weather which makes Melbourne seem like a bloody tropical hothouse!'

England won by 9 wickets. There was no mention by Rivett of any Pakistan bowlers being called for throwing, and there was anecdotal evidence that such a 'throwing truce' had been applied by the MCC to West Indian bowler Charlie Griffith, a notorious thrower, the following year. Relaxing in a bath at Lord's, England bowler Fred Trueman overheard Robbins telling two match umpires 'not – repeat not – to no-ball Charlie Griffith'. Trueman told the

Observer that he could not believe what he was hearing. Some called it diplomacy, he said, but 'I call it a cover up.'

Rivett loved to work over the selection of Australian cricket teams with Bradman, who was variously a state and national administrator and selector for decades after his retirement from first class cricket in 1949. At a state level his involvement in cricket administration via the South Australian Cricket Association (SACA) lasted until 1986, retiring aged seventy-seven, but his participation at national level was cut short, in relative terms, by the World Series Cricket revolution leading to his retirement from the Australian Cricket Board (ACB) in 1980, aged seventy-one.

In early 1964 Rivett complimented the selectors on the make-up of the current Australian team in a letter to Bradman, who agreed with the few critical comments that accompanied the praise. Preoccupied with the shock death of his old friend Len Bullock at the time, Bradman was gentler with Rivett over cricketing matters than he was to be on some other occasions. It was the old story, Bradman said: selectors can only select from the players available. The fast bowlers selected were no cause for particular satisfaction, but the selectors could only choose the best from those playing the game.

Cricket had enjoyed something of a rally early in the decade, with the exciting 1960–61 tour of Australia by the Frank Worrell-captained West Indies facing a well-led Australian team captained by Richie Benaud. The West Indies team included Gary Sobers, Wes Hall and Rohan Kanhai and, for the life of the series, cricket fever once again gripped Australia. The paying crowd for the series approached one million. Australia won the inaugural Frank Worrell Trophy.

But as the 1960s continued, the Australian selectors and administrators came under increasing pressure. The media took a regular stick to the team and the selectors. The Fifth Test between England and Australia in Sydney in February 1963 was an absolute contrast to the thrilling West Indies tour two years earlier. Australia had won back the Ashes on England's 1958–59 tour, and with Australia and England both scoring one win each from the first four Tests, Benaud understandably adopted a more defensive posture than might otherwise have been the case. The Sydney Test was 'one of the most boring tests imaginable,' according to cricket historian Chris Harte: 'When Australia was set 241 to win in 240 minutes, Lawry batted the whole time for 45 runs with the series ending amid jeers and catcalls from the crowd on the Sydney Hill.'

Bradman and Benaud agreed on the question of 'bright cricket'. The question was how to make Australia's increasingly hidebound cricket culture yield to a more positive, dynamic approach. Bradman did his best as an administrator to encourage a new, positive, more modern stance. But turning around the antediluvian apparatus and philosophical decrepitude that was Australian cricket in the 1960s and early 1970s turned out to be more than one man, even one as clever as Bradman, could do.

The media nagging and bagging to which Australian cricket was subjected frustrated Bradman in the extreme. At one point in the correspondence he thanked Rivett for not lecturing him on the game in the letter he had just received. It was welcome respite. The lack of credit Australia received from its own commentators for lifting playing standards in South Africa and New Zealand to the point where they were competitive and could occasionally win a match was an especially sore point: 'The latter is a far far better thing *for cricket* than an Aust. victory.'

As the 1964 Ashes tour of England approached, Bradman told Rivett how much he looked forward to listening to the broadcasts. But he couldn't help feeling that the matches would be dull: 'Outside [Ted] Dexter & perhaps [Norman] O'Neill, where is there to be much gaiety in the batting? And the bowling on both sides seems mediocre & unexciting. Perhaps worse our fielding, expected to be a strong point, has moved the staid McGilvray to strong words.'

The English summer of 1964 was not a wet one as English summers go, and yet three of the five Tests in the series were rain-affected, including the first in June at Trent Bridge – drawn in a wash-out. 'Oh I forgot the other gloomy news – the Test & the Derbyshire game and *Lawry*,' Bradman maundered. 'What a peculiar side we have. Fingers crossed for Lords.'

But the Lord's Test, when it began nine days later, made Trent Bridge seem like balmy weather. Playing time was halved because of the rain. Bill Lawry was bowled by Fred Trueman for 4 in the first innings, then caught by Dexter off a ball from Gifford for 20. Play was abandoned on the final day for a draw when the heavens opened once more. The match led to the installation of new drainage at Lord's after one spectator complained in the letters column of the *Times* that water siphoned by hose from the playing area was being drained back onto other parts of the field which themselves required redraining.

More thoughts on one selection arrived from Rivett, for which Bradman thanked him. He took major issue with Rivett's view of Norman O'Neill, who in Bradman's opinion was Australia's most 'attractive' batsman: 'I am well aware he is inconsistent but you have the job ahead of you to find someone *consistently brilliant* and *also* reliable.'

Bradman was batching during the Ashes tour, and was losing weight and feeling old. He sub-edited part of Rivett's next letter by return mail, telling his friend that he felt 'aged' not 'aging'. Not that he was actually sick, Bradman hastened to add, but he had lost four kilograms due to his mediocre cooking, and possibly to the 'agony of Manchester'.

Benaud had retired as Australian captain prior to the series, and Bob Simpson had assumed the role. With one win and two draws in the first three matches, the Fourth Test at Old Trafford would be decisive providing Australia at least managed a draw. Just as Benaud had done in Australia in the same situation, Simpson played defensively to protect the prize. Simpson scored 311 runs in nearly thirteen hours at the wicket; his opening stand of 201 with Bill Lawry (106) broke the previous opening partnership record set fifty-five years earlier. Australia declared at 656 for 8; England scored 611 with Barrington (256) and Dexter (174) leading the England scorers, and the match was drawn.

Privately Bradman despaired: 'What are you to do when 5 days is barely enough to dismiss each team once,' he asked Rivett. 'This is not in my view, a revelation of lack of bowlers or of batting strength, but a symptom of a mental outlook which is not very healthy for cricket.' The cause was deep rooted, he said, threatening to argue it with Rivett for hours when next they got together.

English cricket was characterised by negativity, Bradman thought, and it not only cruelled their game but dragged down modern cricket overall. Further, he blamed the bodyline series, now more than thirty years in the past, for the palpable 'enmity & grimness' still evident between England and Australia.

'You may say "that's rubbish – modern players weren't born then",' Bradman wrote. 'But they know all about it. Moreover they feel the English "approach" is still basically that they can't face up to losing & so won't take a chance.' In the Old Trafford Test, for example, Dexter would not give Barrington, a handy leg spinner as well as a wonderful batsman, even a single over to bowl in the game: 'Why? Because Dexter will never agree to "buy" a wicket. Their selections are always based on defence – off spin bowlers who are tight and so on. Why did Graveney . . . so often get passed over? Because they said he played shots. Too risky.'

Bradman accused the English press of bias, calling their roasting of Simpson one sided after the Australian captain declared before lunch on the third day at Old Trafford 656 for 8. He looked at 'Wisden 1938' to see what England had done in similar circumstances in the Fourth Test at The Oval in 1938. England declared at 903 for 7 – at tea on the third day. In the clincher, Bradman quoted the Wisden editor: 'Hammond probably would *not* have closed the innings during the tea interval on the 3rd day but for the mishap to the opposing Captain.' Bradman had broken his ankle and Jack Fingleton had pulled a muscle, so Australia only had nine players to bat – 'or if you like – 8 plus Fleetwood Smith', he quipped.

Always one to enjoy dry wit, Bradman broke the spirited defence of Simpson against Fleet Street's unfairness to recount an anecdote from the 1938 game in which the Australians were so stricken, and which England won by an innings and 579 runs. The England wicketkeeper, Arthur Ward, was a Yorkshireman. He came in to bat with England at 6 for 770, made 53 and was out with England at 7 for 876. Bradman told Rivett: 'As he went up the pavilion steps a member said "well played Arthur". In a flash he replied "Thanks – I'm always at my best in a crisis".'

Arthur Ward's wit did not keep Bradman long from his private onslaught against England's lack of attacking attitude. Ted Dexter was a serial offender, in his view, and he cited the Fifth Test in England's most recent tour of Australia as evidence. England *had* to win that deciding match to retrieve the Ashes. 'But what did Dexter do after promising us all he would play cricket – he instructed his players just to stay there.' England scored 195 the first day, Barrington's 101 took an agonisingly long 320 minutes and Trueman was at the wicket for 110 minutes 'without hitting or trying to hit a four'. Then England pegged Australia down with three off spinners. Until the English changed their approach 'our chaps will continue to re-act adversely and of course it is bad for the game'.

But as deeply as Bradman despaired, he urged his friend to dwell on the positive, not the negative. 'Remember how the West Indies filled the MCG & I hope they'll do it again,' he wrote. 'They are an attraction now whereas 30 years ago few people went to see them play.'

Occasionally Rivett would send Bradman the draft of a freelance article on cricket for comment before placing the piece, usually with the *Age* or the *Canberra Times*. It was lucky he had a robust personality because Bradman was merciless on his special subject when Rivett stirred his critical faculties with arguable assertions.

One such case was a long draft article Rivett sent in 1964,

looking backwards to how good cricket had once been and trying to draw lessons from the past which might make it great again. Bradman replied, at length, that in him Rivett's arguments had stirred 'misgivings'. There were 'elements of truth' in it, but only some of the judgements were justified and some of the comparisons made were, to Bradman, not fair.

A key element in the piece concerned declining cricket attendance in Australia, about which there was considerable concern. Rivett had evidently indulged in some purple prose. 'Your far fetched reference to the "open downs where men still ploughed" when Woolley batted, is pure journalistic license,' Bradman wrote. 'So too your exaggeration of attendances & enthusiasm when Bradman batted. I played before many poor audiences . . . [and the] record crowd is in the 1960s – not the 1930s.' A vast number of competing attractions had emerged, Bradman argued. In the 1920s there was no radio or television, and only a handful of cars with which people busied themselves. Besides, he said, not every player in every era was going to be a cricket great.

Rivett may well have felt like a bowler being hit all over the park by Bradman at the height of his power – but Bradman was just beginning. One by one he took on and dismissed a score of Rivett's arguments. Rivett lamented the loss of leg fields; Bradman said while he had often played against seven, there were no leg fields in the 1960s because the law of cricket now restricted them to five. Rivett worried about the lack of slow spinners like Mailey or F. Smith, but Bradman asked what were Philpott and Sellers if not slow leg spinners? Bradman was on weaker ground dismissing major one-day competitions like the Gillette Cup conducted in Britain. They were a 'gimmick' he argued, and if played intensively would end up being seen as exhibition cricket, not a true contest.

But Bradman was back on the attack over Rivett's suggestion to save money by cutting Sheffield Shield games from four days to three. When South Australia travelled to play in Queensland, New South Wales and Victoria, three-day matches instead of four would save just one day – the last – in the three weeks of the trip overall.

Another Rivett suggestion, limiting innings by number of overs or by a time limit, had been tried and found wanting by district cricket associations throughout Australia, according to Bradman. It simply created too powerful an incentive for defensive tactics. In fact, Bradman had driven the adoption of a new points system in Australia where clubs got no points at all for a draw; to get points a team had to both dismiss their opponent *and* get more runs.

Nor was Rivett's suggestion that there should be a crackdown on bowling 18 inches outside the stumps likely to be effective since it had virtually disappeared anyway, not least because it was easier for batsmen to deal with 'than the stuff which is bang on your middle & leg all the time – like Titmus'.

There were indeed problems, Bradman agreed. But his diagnosis was negativity, inadequacy, over-coaching and a surfeit of cricket breeding familiarity, and in turn contempt, among the media. His view of the evils of over-coaching, of taking the natural flair and excitement from a player's personal style, was especially interesting: 'The great & attractive stars were not coached. The atavistic approach of Sobers would drive a coach to drink – but the spectators love it. Too much cricket, radio etc(?) may be breeding an air of contempt – familiarity. Newspapers are too prone to criticise & condemn – loathe to praise.'

Richie Benaud's old team, Cumberland, had scored more than 400 runs in four hours playing Paddington a few days earlier, something the press had totally ignored. But Bradman guaranteed the media would not miss the opportunity to attack Western Australia for slow scoring in a recent game.

Cricket would ebb and flow, and there would be some adjustments, but cricket was too complex and valuable to have to absorb critiques that did not at the same time lift the game. Like Rivett, Bradman felt low at times about the state of the game. But he urged Rohan to cheer up: they would both continue to love the game and get their share of pleasant surprises about it: 'Like the boy who wrote me yesterday & said "I'm aged 11 & I've admired you ever since I was young".'

One impending pleasure was Australia's tour of the West Indies the following year, 1965. The warm-up matches in Kingston, Jamaica had unfolded the way Bradman had anticipated, but he knew the Tests themselves would follow their own course: 'Taking all things into a/c I imagine we shall be extremely hard pressed but it will be no pushover for either side.'

The West Indies won the First Test at Sabina Park, by 179 runs. Charlie Griffith was clearly throwing, the Australian team believed, but no umpire called him on it. In the Second Test, in Port-of-Spain, Trinidad, Bradman reported with pleasure on Australia's fightback. 'I hope they don't run out of X-Ray plates for O'Neill,' he quipped after Norman O'Neill was hit on the arm by a Griffith delivery while trying to protect his head. The match was a draw, followed by an Australian loss in the Third Test in Georgetown, Guyana, and a draw in the Fourth Test in Barbados. A victorious West Indies claimed the Frank Worrell Trophy.

In the run-up to and during this mid-1960s period, anachronism upon anachronism had been dealt to Australian cricketers who, while living and playing in the modern era, were paid and treated as though it was half a century earlier. The players came under minute and virtually absolute control by the ruling national body – the Australian Board of Control, later renamed the Australian Cricket Board (ACB) – leading to a range of arcane and oppressive restrictions. They were paid a pittance, and first grade players not infrequently cut short their cricket careers because the financial sacrifice required was too much. In terms of internal relations, board members lived on high and looked down on the players like so many serfs beneath them, or so it seemed to an increasingly disgruntled group of Australian players.

More than most, Bradman was alert to the dangers of grandiose perceptions of self-worth. Personal, but not false, modesty had been a conscious keynote in Bradman since, as a thirteen year old, he had first watched Johnny Taylor play. He had observed the ill-effects of egotism in others. Around this time he and Rivett had an exchange about England's Ted Dexter concerning a fan of Dexter's who had worked diligently to get him onto the England team. 'Ted lapped that up,' Bradman commented. 'But having got there he imagined himself to be a god.'

Bradman did not think that he, Bradman, was a god despite being the one cricketer who might be half-forgiven for flirting with the idea. The same could not necessarily be said for some other members of the ACB or for its institutional personality, which was autocratic and imperious. Bradman was but one voice and vote among many on the ACB, he often reminded Rivett, just as when he was a selector his was only one of three views which led to selections being made. Getting onto the ACB was something of a Byzantine exercise in itself, and cricket administrators who set out on the long, tortuous path that was involved tended not to be talented players from the game's elite level, let alone with international experience.

Bradman was an exception, and he was a force for progress. '[As] always, there was one man eating away at the old guard's philosophy, one man who knew how to handle them and yet keep the new breed in check while old fortresses slowly crumbled,' as cricket historian Chris Harte has commented. 'What Australian cricket owes to Don Bradman is inestimable.' But the things Bradman was doing to try and nudge the ACB out of the dark ages and get more 'bright cricket' played – and there were many – were not on a scale and speed anything like that building up to engulf traditional cricket in the 1970s. The ACB was like the boiling frog in the classic management parable: the one in the water where the temperature is rising so gradually that the frog doesn't register until it is already half-cooked that the water is nearly boiling.

There were so many immediate challenges and crises to deal with. In October 1965 Rivett warned Bradman about the developing situation in Rhodesia and South Africa. Bradman told Rivett that his assessment frightened him, but he nevertheless (and for the time being correctly) clung to the view that cricket fixtures in South Africa were not yet about to be disrupted in an anti-colonial or racial war. He acknowledged, though, that his instinct was based on nothing more than that 'often of late a war has been in the offing but at the crucial moment the contestants seem to pull back from the brink of a holocaust'. Of concern right at that instant, in any case, was an imminent England Ashes tour. Bradman wanted a successful series but told Rivett this depended on the English approach: 'We will meet them half way if they approach the game in the right spirit but if they don't our fellows won't be suckers.'

Intelligent, stubborn, well-travelled and imbued with his own abiding love for cricket, Rivett was not about to let Bradman's point-by-point rebuffing of his earlier thoughts on what could be done end his quest to improve things. In late 1965 Rivett wrote to Victorian administrator Ray Steele about what might be done to strengthen cricket's base in Australia.

> I have given considerable thought to the problems you posed at the MCG on Monday over the past year or two. Therefore I was very delighted to find that Bill Dowling, yourself and others had decided to take some action before cricket becomes one of those minority games largely played and patronised by a faithful few. I do not think you can blame the newspapers. On the whole newspapers and radio – both ABC here and BBC in Britain – have done cricket quite proudly – even more so since the advent of television.
>
> Go back to first principles and apply the lessons I learned on the two Boards on which I served for a decade in South Australia, I am sure it's a case of 'you have to catch 'em young'.
>
> Over the last fifteen years the tiny island of Barbados with a population much smaller than Melbourne has produced as many *great* cricketers as the other seven cricket playing nations. Why? In part because every youngster is encouraged in his first grades at school and thereafter to play on the pitches provided in every yard and park. On the

Savannah in the heart of Port of Spain you can see more than 70 matches going on simultaneously at any free hour in the summer. In Bombay, along Marine Drive, I have counted more than 3,000 cricketers actively engaged at one time on well prepared pitches in matches and practice.

It may be a false premise but I believe there is not nearly enough liaison between yourselves as cricket authorities and the schools. I am *not* talking about the great Public Schools or their senior teams.

It is probably too late this last week in November to make the revolutionary step of taking 2,000, or even 1,000 seats at the MCG for every day (barring Saturday if you like) of the 2nd test, December 30–January 4. But it would be a splendid beginning to invite 50 Primary Schools, inside and outside the metropolitan area, to nominate 20 chosen youngsters . . . to be the guests of the VCA for one day of a Test Match, to sit in a block, widely publicised, photographed *and* televised, as the VCA Schoolboy Test Seats . . .

Before you blanch at the financial side of this promotion, one should point out that at Georgetown, Barbados, for the 4th Test there were 5,000 school children *seated* each day in a reserve stand built exclusively for school children. If the West Indies Cricket Association or the Barbados Club can afford to promote cricket with its youngsters on that scale, we, with our far greater affluence, in a city of two million should at least be able to find 1,000 seats for our youngsters.

The letter continued for another two pages, and was followed by another principally concerned with bowling rates, this time sent to three other administrators as well as Bradman and Ray Steele. Bradman replied at the beginning of December, and said he looked forward to discussing it. In the meantime he wanted to explain the arrangements in different states that already existed to help young cricketers get seats at fixtures. He wanted to set things straight about the West Indies too. The West Indies paid the Australian team's expenses for the tour but kept all the profit. It was different in Australia, he pointed out. Bradman was not closing out the dialogue on what might be done – just adding empirical information to it.

Six weeks later, in January 1966, he found himself unable to get hold of Rivett. Bradman had rung him in Sydney, where the Third Test in the latest Ashes series was played, but there was no Rivett and no response to Bradman's message asking him to get in touch: 'Perhaps you were as despondent as I was about the cricket & couldn't face me.' Australia had lost to England by an innings and 93 runs. But there was no breach.

Later in the year Rivett sought advice on the bowling of his son Keith. Bradman told him Keith should pursue accuracy, not pace: learn accuracy until it is automatic. Most wickets fall to batting errors, he pointed out; meanwhile, the bowler's job was to contain the run rate through accurate bowling. It was like playing the piano, said Bradman (who was also an accomplished pianist): 'Practise the right notes enough and a wrong one becomes a rarity.' Legendary bowler Bill O'Reilly took 7 overs per wicket, so expecting to do better than that would be unrealistic. The trick was to contain the run rate to around 3 an over, otherwise one's averages would blow out.

In November 1966 Bradman told Rivett to mark his little black book with the name of Ian Chappell's younger brother, Greg, who had just made 53 in his Shield debut for South Australia at just eighteen years old. Unless he was a bad judge, wrote Bradman, 'here is a lad to watch'.

Despite the various problems facing Australian cricket, Bradman was rather jovial. He cracked jokes with Rivett about the latter's insatiable appetite for trying to influence the selection process. 'As usual I lapped up all your "advice" on our cricketers,' Bradman wrote in late November. 'We won't pick the team you want for NZ but then poor old DGB will be outvoted again. It won't be a bad side all the same.' And then again in his next letter, Bradman thanked Rivett for further advice before reiterating that he had only one selector's vote in three and that he did not determine the batting order: 'And if I disagree with the published verdict of the selection committee, you would have as much chance of knowing it as I would have if [Adelaide *News* editor Ron] Boland wrote a leader [with which he disagreed] under the direction of R.M.' 'R.M.' was, of course, Rupert Murdoch.

In June Bradman recounted the goings-on of the 'Peanut Dinner' where Paul Sheahan was named 'Cricketer of the Year'. Vic Richardson, a legendary player and grandfather of Ian, Greg and Trevor Chappell, began his speech at the event by saying it was right to call on him since he'd been playing for peanuts all his life. But there was a 'PS': Bradman asked Rivett to check on the quiet whether the news on the grapevine was true that a particular cricketer and his room-mate were hitting the grog. He may have to make some decisions affecting the cricketers' futures, he said, and wanted to have the full picture.

The pressure occasionally began to show on Bradman, and in such situations even Rohan wasn't immune from a stiff serve.

Bradman's heavy program had apparently got him down. On top of his normal commitments he had just spent time helping the Wally Hammond Memorial Appeal, and writing a contribution to a book honouring the former Indian test captain Vizianagram, who was about to turn sixty. The next day the press reported 'Vizzy' had died of a heart attack the previous night '. . . and the mail brings your epistle, thrashing me about 6-8 ball overs, Doble v Johnston, overs bowled per hours etc'.

Rivett's letter was 'full of anomalies & I'm just in the mood to bash you down', he wrote. 'Anyone with half an eye can see that there is about as much resemblance between Doble & Bill Johnston as between Bradman and Larwood.' He conceded to some exaggeration, but it conveyed his point. 'As for the 6 and 8 ball over question, this is not worth wasting time on.' He then proceeded with a detailed rebuttal of the argument that 6 ball overs would speed the game up.

If fast bowlers were on one would probably get more balls bowled with 6 ball overs, but if slow bowlers were on the situation would be reversed. Bradman cited the mean average of the bowling rate on Australia's 1960 tour of New Zealand, where 6 ball overs were played: balls per minute (6 ball) averaged 1.898. The mean average for the whole 1960–61 Australian season (8 ball) was 1.886. 'In a 5 hour day the different amounted to *3 balls*,' he wrote. The impact was likely to be negligible, Bradman argued, contrary to the claims of some.

Bradman had got the scoring rate per 100 balls bowled for every test series in the twentieth century and said it was unlikely that anyone else in the world had done so. The figures showed how 'stupid' a lot of the press criticism on the issue was:

England	1902 – 45	1953 – 44
Australia	1902 – 44	1955 – 45

Rohan's claim that spectators were now seeing one-third less play than they used to was wrong, Bradman continued. It was true at times under Hutton's leadership of England, and that was 'disgraceful'. But really it came down to who was bowling, the time they took and so on. One couldn't force a bowler to take a 5 yard run-up instead of 15, and if one laid down a maximum run-up, bowlers with shorter run-ups would tend to boost theirs up to the maximum: 'Besides you would make sure we never again saw the beauty of Wes Hall.'

The fire in Bradman's belly on such matters was undiminished. However, former Test batsman Neil Harvey's imminent arrival as a selector in 1967, which Bradman supported, made him ponder how much longer he could or should go on. 'It increasingly becomes a tie and surely I have long since repaid cricket what it did for me,' he confided in Rivett. 'Perhaps I can render service a little longer but I am not one who would wish to hold the stage when a better replacement was available.'

In October 1967 Bradman went to Perth, which he loved. Despite being 'tired as hell' from the trip, he dashed off a note to Rivett, partly to thank him for drawing his attention to a compliment for him from C.P. Snow. 'But alas I was referred to as the great *English* cricketer,' Bradman joshed. 'I almost swooned. Yes I've seen it & appreciate the undeserved compliment.'

Bradman was struck with the contrast between Adelaide and Perth. Even the cricket was better there, he claimed. Bradman told Rivett he had seen a great match in Perth, the word 'great' underlined twice, with the list of possible selections for Australia growing. He even got to congratulate Bill Lawry on risking everything in a bid to win: 'That is really something – a great change in outlook.' Bradman also congratulated English bowler Tony Lock, then playing Sheffield Shield in Australia, on getting Bitmead out – and on getting a ball to turn for the first time: 'He nearly punched my nose, but as the joke sank in he shouted me a beer instead. Fine captaincy.'

For a man of trenchant views, Bradman was disarming in his ability to admit he was wrong about something. His view that a bowler couldn't drag until his front foot was on the ground was one of his biggest errors in cricket, he told Rivett in August 1968. Bradman thought bowlers need a 'fulcrum' to support the slide. Film of bowlers in action, especially the Australian quick Gordon Rorke and English fast bowler Fred Trueman, 'made a monkey out of that statement', he said. In the Fourth Test in Adelaide in 1959, Rorke dragged his right foot a few yards when unleashing the ball.

At the same time, he could not understand why others, especially the media, could so stubbornly argue positions that were simply not right. Australia's 1968 Ashes tour was nearly over and the Australian media were thrashing the team. Of the four tests already played, Australia had won one and drawn three matches. The Second Test at Lord's saw Australia dismissed for 78 in the first innings, with Walters top-scoring on 26 followed by Gleeson on 14; Lawry and Jarman were out for ducks and everyone else was on single figures. In the Fourth Test at Headingley, which England had to win in order to keep its Ashes hopes alive, the Australians got a pasting from the media even though it was England that had played defensively when Australian teams in a similar position in the past had gone for it. What is more, if Bradman came out publicly and told the world that Australia had been trying to win, desperately so, he wouldn't be believed he told Rivett – and besides, the damage from the publicity had been done and in his view couldn't be undone.

It upset Bradman that people based their views on cricket so heavily on what was written about it, and journalists seemed bent on criticism whatever actually transpired. At Headingley the Australians, and Bradman singled out Ian Chappell as an example, were attacked by the media for not scoring fast enough to win: 'But at the Oval, when Chappell tried to do just that but got caught behind, he was roasted for a rash shot and for not having the application of Mallett. It is just plain bloody stupid. You can't have it both ways. If a chap is expected to try and attack he must not be condemned if in trying to do just that he fails.'

The one-all result of the 1968 tour of England, with Australia retaining the Ashes, was a reasonable reflection of the teams' abilities, Bradman thought. But he hoped the West Indies tour of Australia in the coming summer would liven things up.

The media, however, was sceptical and unforgiving. A leader in the *Age* one Saturday at the end of August 1968 was headlined 'Is Don Bradman Out?' It gave no benefit of doubt to the Australian team or Australian cricket generally:

> As this is the day before the day of rest, and a pretty restful day itself, it seems the right time to be philosophical. We have had little opportunity recently; what with Czechoslovakia, the Chicago anguish, the Calwellian doctrine of perpetual incumbency, and omnipresent Vietnam. The subject is

> cricket, and a very serious subject it is. It would be a gross dishonesty to say 'we have been moved to write about cricket' because the cricket we have experienced in the past few months has been so dull as to leave cricketers motionless, far less editorial writers. We really want to offer a lament, a lament for Anglo-Australian Tests in particular and for cricket in general. The Test series just ended may not have killed cricket but, Lord protect us, it has excavated the grave.

What, the *Age* wanted to know, had happened to cricket? The players had stopped playing, the leader said, answering its own rhetorical question. Three of the five Ashes Tests in England had been 'absurdities' where 'when rain did not stop play, the players did'. Australia was overly defensive and England, requiring dash and imagination to seize the prize, instead 'played the game like ladies at croquet'. Neither side appeared convinced of its own powers, and the series was deservedly tied since neither side deserved to win. The game itself was the loser according to the editorial. 'So let us not congratulate ourselves on saving the Ashes,' it said. '[The] way this past series way played, sackcloth would be more appropriate.' Like Bradman, the *Age* looked forward to the West Indies team's arrival to inject vim back into the game over the Australian summer.

Nineteen sixty-eight was a wild year in the wider world. The May riots in Paris unofficially constituted the New Left's breakthrough moment in the 1960s counterculture 'revolution'. The reverberations of the previous year's 'summer of love' in the US was rolling through other western nations. Cricket may have seemed impervious but, in fact, the first seeds of dissent were sprouting on multiple fronts. Cricket's key symbolic role in the fight over apartheid in South Africa was about to emerge; player discontent over their earnings from cricket was on the horizon; and player behaviour on the ground, especially in relation to language, began its decline.

Coloured London-based South African cricketer Basil D'Oliveira had hit a creditable 158 for England in the Fifth Test against Australia in August 1968 and bowled Barry Jarman at a critical point in the match. He was subsequently selected for the England team for the Test series against South Africa. The South African government, however, banned him from touring, leading to the cessation of cricket competition between the two nations. 'Like you I feel a bit sick about S.Africa, simply because of its effect on the game,' Bradman wrote to Rivett. About who and what were to blame for the breakdown in relations he was uncertain from Adelaide's far climes, but he intended meeting with the president of the South African cricket board, who was visiting Adelaide, to find out.

At the conclusion of Australia's Ashes tour, many team members begged off flying straight home in favour of staying in England to play remunerative sponsored games. According to cricket historian Chris Harte: 'The next meeting of the Board . . . saw Sir Donald Bradman, surprisingly perhaps, ask the question "If the players wanted shorter official tours of England, then why are they prepared to extend their time away from home by playing in sponsored games?"' It was a clear sign of the yawning gap between Bradman's perceptions of player earnings and the players' own perceptions – a chasm that would have major consequences for Australian cricket over the following decade.

There were so many micro aspects of the game, though, that

demanded and absorbed attention. In November 1968 Bradman related his fascination at the generally lowly Queensland beating New South Wales, the doyen of cricketing states then languishing, by an innings in a recent Shield game. He reported that his 'patient prodding' had led to the best wicket on the Sydney Cricket Ground (SCG) for a generation, with Western Australia batting magnificently at the ground as a result. Bradman's close, continuing efforts to standardise and improve the rules of cricket continued. 'And almost miraculously,' he told Rivett, 'the former Secy of MCC & the incoming President [have] now publicly supported the LBW rule I've wanted since 1932. Ye Gods – what a victory.' Was Rohan still coming over for the West Indies Test against Australia in Adelaide, he wanted to know. They were not as strong as they had been in 1961, he thought, 'but are we?' Australia eventually prevailed.

One struggle in which Bradman never prevailed was that with his old test cricket team-mate Jack Fingleton. Fingleton had spent years chipping away at Bradman's reputation and Bradman's anger was palpable. In March 1969 Fingleton wrote from the Canberra press gallery to Rivett asking him 'to run your gifted eye' over a collection of his cricket writings that were to be published as a book, as an input into the editorial process. Rivett had forwarded the letter to Bradman for comment.

Bradman replied quickly, returning Fingleton's letter to Rivett: 'Like his bloody cheek . . .' It did turn Bradman's mind to books he could write if he wanted, not that he would ever be prepared to breach the confidences he possessed. A book on selectors' secrets would be a hit, he thought: 'Gosh it would open some eyes.'

Later in 1969 cricket became a life and death matter during Australia's riot-plagued tour of India. Bradman told Rivett that his 'forebodings make me shudder'; Bradman's reply implies that Rivett had cited communist agitation as a factor in the prevailing political scene in India. In the First Test in Bombay Australian cricketer Johnny Gleeson was hit by a bottle and Bill Lawry had a chair thrown at him from a pavilion balcony; at the Fourth Test at Eden Gardens crowd rioting resulted in six dead, the police being pelted with stones, and the hotel where the Australians were staying being invaded. Would Rivett like his job as chairman of the Australian Board of Control when, he speculated, news came through that Bill Lawry had been killed in a melee? This did not happen but Lawry, in fact, kicked up a storm in the tour's wake about the dangers the Australian team had faced and the inadequacy of Indian cricket authorities to deal with it. Countries which could not keep things under control would have a tough time attracting good teams in the future, Bradman said. 'We'll do our best to keep the cricket flag flying,' he wrote, 'but the communists won't really be interested & if the Chinese or the Russians ever decide they want a slice of this part of the world I rather fancy the Aust. XI won't stand in the way.'

The old order continued to wither, sometimes literally, as the 1960s drew to a close. Victor Richardson died during the Australian tour of India in October 1969. Fourteen years Bradman's senior, the later stages of Richardson's career as a batsman overlapped with Bradman's extraordinary rise. They both endured the devastating England attack of the bodyline series, and coexisted in South Australian cricket circles for more than thirty years after Bradman moved to Adelaide in 1935.

Richardson was a brilliant natural athlete with a swashbuckling style and a close team orientation. The spirit of the Richardson–Bradman relationship can perhaps be summed up in the juxtaposition of two images from an Australian exhibition tour of North America in 1932. Visiting MGM in Hollywood, a group photo with some of the studio's stars has a moustachioed, brilliantined Vic Richardson looking like a film star himself, arm in arm with Mary Astor and Jean Harlow. Bradman looks jockey-like by comparison, tucked away in obscurity behind them. But cricket writer Ray Robinson recounts that some of the exhibition team's toughest matches were against Harlem, a team featuring many migrants from the West Indies, played on rough, gravelly ground. 'Negro barrackers were clamouring to see "Massa Don",' according to Robinson, 'so Vic turned to Bradman, saying "Put the pads on, Massa Don, it's your show".'

There were frictions, both stylistic and generational, between Richardson and Bradman. Harte reports that underlying tensions in 1935 over the Australian and South Australian captaincies, in an episode classically mishandled by administrators, triggered deep animosity in Richardson towards Bradman: 'Richardson went to South Africa spawning hatred of Bradman, and found a number of like minds among his touring colleagues.' Nor were the two men's approaches to life on tour sympathetic. Harte quotes Richardson's grandson, Ian Chappell, recalling advice prior to Chappell's own first tour of South Africa in 1965: 'He took me into the kitchen at home and reminded me of his tour to South Africa in 1935–36. He looked me straight in the eye and said: "Be careful of the women over there. Some of them could be your cousins".'

Rivett wrote about Richardson on his death and forwarded the article to Bradman. 'Despite his faults (which became fewer as he got older) Vic. *was* a great man in so many respects,' Bradman replied. Bradman went to his funeral. Adelaide Oval wouldn't be the same without him, he thought.

Bradman picked Rivett up on one aspect of the piece, however, where he had written that alone Richardson and McCabe had 'defied' bodyline. This was a bit much given his own figures for the series and that he, Bradman, had been the prime target. The implied criticism was a 'bit rough', Bradman thought – or was he being too sensitive, he queried.

Later correspondence that November saw Rivett clear up the perceived offence regarding Bradman and bodyline. Bradman accepted it, while reiterating that he wouldn't have raised the issue had Rivett only referred to the Sydney Test in which Bradman hadn't played. But since Rivett's comment had appeared to apply to the series, he said, his complaint was fair enough. He didn't dwell on it long, though. An exciting Sheffield Shield match between South Australia and Western Australia was of greater interest: 'We had them whacked all the way until after tea on the last day when an idiotic Cunningham ran Greg Chappell out & the rest showed as many cricket brains as a hen.' Sunday play had recently been introduced with a bit of shepherding from Bradman against considerable opposition on the Board of Control. It had gone well, he told Rivett, despite hot northerly winds and a temperature in the mid-thirties.

Things were hotter still in India where the Australian tour continued to attract rioting. The team was surviving all right, he reported. Never mind Richie Benaud's 'impassioned plea' for the tourists to leave: 'He didn't seem to mind risking his own neck to go there with the Cavaliers but I guess that was different. He was being paid. Now he is being paid to criticise.'

In the early 1970s Bradman's biggest challenge yet as an administrator awaited him: cricketing relations with South Africa, against which international activism over apartheid was intensifying. He believed British Prime Minister Harold Wilson, who lost office in the 1970 general election, had sacrificed votes by pressing for the abandonment of England's Test series with South Africa. That episode was over, he told Rivett; the question he then posed his friend was what should be done about South Africa's proposed tour of Australia in the summer of 1971–72.

The fact that Bradman seriously sought Rivett's view was interesting given that Rivett was perceived to be just a few shades this side of a red-ragger in his politics. Instead of a harangue, Rivett's reply was exemplary and Bradman's praise by return mail unstinting. Rivett might not believe it to be the case, he wrote, but he had always respected Rohan's opinion and given it due weight. He had only discounted it when Rivett appeared rash or hasty in his judgement, or was being stubborn 'for the sake of being bloody minded or provoking an argument', including on subjects where Bradman was better acquainted with the facts – namely cricket.

'But let me come off my bike and say your letter of July 3rd [1970] about Africa was the best letter you have ever written me because it was a calm, considered, reasoned survey of something where you really know more than most people,' Bradman wrote to his friend. 'You appeared to try and persuade me as Chairman of the Board what was in our best interests – not tell me what we had to do. Just let me say how much I appreciated it.'

Rivett's letter is not included in the series but Bradman's tendency to respond seriatim provides a good guide to its content.

Rivett first canvassed the cricket considerations for and against a South African tour of Australia that summer. Three favoured the tour, and there was one against. Then he reflected the non-cricket considerations affecting the decision. 'So let's get down to some candid speaking,' Bradman declared in reply. He told Rivett he thought the three cricket considerations favouring the tour were 'valid but to my mind not important' compared to the other issues; and he thought the one cricket issue Rivett raised against it 'important', though he wondered whether Rivett was overestimating the likely hostility from young Australians to the tour. 'But,' came the rider, 'you may be much nearer the truth than I.'

Bradman then dealt with the other factors Rivett had raised – firstly his proposal that there be no further test matches against South Africa until all its citizens were eligible to play. Bradman observed that this would mean the next summer's tour was off, as all others would be until the South African government passed legislation to end apartheid in cricket. Bradman told Rivett he thought this would ultimately happen, but not in the foreseeable future. He agreed with Rivett that students and trade unionists would disrupt the tour if it went ahead.

Recognising Rivett was correct about people's dislike of the situation in South Africa, Bradman nevertheless questioned whether it was different in principle from the oppression under other regimes like that of the Soviet Union and other countries with whom Australia traded and played sport. He argued that the South African Cricket Association was not responsible for apartheid, and that it had tried to give 50 000 rand to the 'Non-white Cricket Association', which refused to accept it.

The Australian police would find it hard to control the

situation, Bradman agreed, and if the unions chose to dig in over the tour there was no way to stop them. He did not like it: 'I find it repugnant to accept the situation that a citizen can be prevented from doing a lawful and harmless thing by someone who disagrees.'

Opinion on the subcontinent also had to be considered, Bradman said: 'The Asian view is of course important and due weight must be given to it.' Not that there was potentially much cricket at stake at the time. Australia's last mooted tour of Pakistan had been cancelled; future tours of India were under a cloud because of the rioting during the previous one, and there were fundamental disagreements over the gate-taking splits. India's most recent Test in Adelaide had yielded a $4000 loss yet the Indian cricket authorities wanted guarantees of the same profits from tours of Australia as they enjoyed from Australian Test tours of India. 'The circumstances are not remotely comparable,' he wrote.

Rivett concluded in his letter that there should be no tour. Without committing himself, Bradman asked Rivett what he should do as chairman of the ACB if he were to come to the same conclusion – and what he should do if, in that position, he was outvoted.

Whatever decision he took, Bradman felt he was in line for ridicule from a large section of the Australian community. So he asked Rivett to put himself in Bradman's shoes and explain how he would handle the situation. 'This is by far the worst thing I've ever been confronted with in cricket and I make no bones about it, I want help and guidance,' Bradman wrote. 'What you say I'll listen to and digest very deeply.'

It was unprecedented in the correspondence for Bradman to put so much reliance on Rivett, especially since it was a matter on which Rivett could be virtually guaranteed to take an especially progressive stance. Even as he did so, however, implicitly acknowledging that he was likely to reach the same conclusion as Rivett, his mind drew him back to the seeming inconsistency that could involve. In a long postscript he pointed out that the Chinese had just released a western bishop who had been imprisoned for eleven years, but Australia still sold the Chinese wheat; and that Soviet soccer players were still welcome in Australia despite Soviet troops mowing down women and children in Prague: 'Aren't the wires crossed somewhere?'

Rivett's analysis and advice proved influential. In September 1971 the Australian Board of Control announced that it believed it was in the best interests of Australia and of cricket that the South African tour not proceed. The official statement cited consultation with 'responsible Australian authorities' including political leaders, union officials, church officials, police commissioners, ground authorities and administrators on the issue. The conclusion drawn was that considerable internal bitterness would be generated and that large-scale demonstrations were inevitable. The invitation was withdrawn.

> The Board wishes to commend the South African Cricket Association and its players for their courageous stand against their Government's apartheid policy in cricket.
>
> It earnestly hopes that the South African Government will in the near future so relax its laws that the cricketers of South Africa may once again take their place as full participants in the international field and the Board will give its utmost support to the South African Cricket Association to try and bring about this end.

The Board organised at short notice an alternative World XI series against Australia to replace the South African Tests, with the ring-in team captained by West Indian legend Sir Garfield Sobers producing some stunning cricket. The side comprised two more West Indians, three South Africans, three Pakistanis, three Indians, a New Zealander and four Englishmen. It was truly, as the anti-apartheid activist and later South Australian premier John Bannon has observed, a 'rainbow' side.

Rivett continued to advise Bradman through that tumultuous period in 1971. In September, as the stress of the decision climaxed and subsided, Rivett apparently suggested some rest might be in order. Bradman told his friend that he knew he was right but that he had to proceed with his program: 'This World XI is one hell of an exercise in diplomacy & detail . . .' What was more, Don and Jessie had to go to New Zealand together in November to fulfil a promise of eight years' standing to give a speech in aid of crippled children for the Murray Halberg Trust. The next four months would be difficult, he said, but after that he could see some 'daylight'.

Later that month Rivett wrote again, praising him for the way the issue of the South African tour had been handled. Bradman thanked him for the letter, including the compliments, but said that – 'no offence meant' – elation was not really his mood in the aftermath. He had seen so much from both perspectives on the issue, 'the good and the bad of each', and told Rivett he was not meant for politics or banner carrying: 'Have you ever stopped to think how much the hurly burly and turmoil of cricket have taken out of me in the last 40 years? All this has been fate, when a simple country lad wanted nothing more than to play cricket for fun and as a joy and recreation and loved the simple life in the country with birds and animals. What has happened to me has been by accident; thrust upon me if you like.'

He told Rivett he couldn't understand the inner life of someone like then federal Opposition Leader Gough Whitlam, whom Bradman perceived as a powermonger who revelled in publicity. In his occasional triumphs in the 'modest arena' in which he had striven, Bradman told Rivett he had been drawn to solitude and quietude. Yet public attention, to his despair, he acknowledged was apparently his fate: 'Perhaps my reward will come posthumously for I guess historians will assess whether I faithfully served mankind.'

In mid-1972 the dialogue on selection continued between the two men. Cricket had been interesting, Bradman said in the wake of the Second Test at Lord's – known as 'Massie's Match'. In the wake of a First Test loss to England at Old Trafford, Western Australia's Bob Massie blitzed England taking 8 for 84 in 32.5 overs with his controlled swing bowling in the first innings, followed by 8 for 53 in the second. Australia won by eight wickets. Bradman told Rivett once again that while he may not have picked exactly the team then touring England, how could he know if his own pick would have performed any better?

Australia had a decent chance on the 1972 Ashes tour because of youth and good fielding, among other things, he thought. The Ian Chappell-captained squad included Stackpole, Francis, Greg Chappell, Walters, Edwards, Gleeson, Marsh, Colley, Massie and Lillee. Rivett had questioned Walters' indifferent performance: he had been caught Illingworth, bowled Snow, for one in the first innings; the match was won before he got the chance to bat in the second. 'Marvellous ability but lack of application,' was Bradman's verdict.

Jack Fingleton again wrote to Rivett from the Canberra press gallery, asking him another favour – this time a request he review Fingleton's latest cricket book for the *Canberra Times*, which often took pieces by Rivett from Melbourne. 'I don't mind how you whack it,' Fingleton wrote, 'so long as my fellow Australians know that I do write on cricket and especially in Canberra, where I have many cobbers.'

Rivett shared the request with Bradman who inadvertently, but with potent symbolism, caught his paperknife in Fingleton's letter, slashing it. That was what the letter deserved, Bradman told Rivett, but since Rivett had asked for it back Bradman painstakingly retyped and returned it. The accompanying letter was excoriating about Fingleton: an outpouring dammed up by years of remaining mute in the face of Fingleton's slights against him, Fingleton's own former Australian team-mate and captain.

Cricket writer Ray Robinson referred to arrows directed at Bradman 'from the untiring bows of a couple of ex-player writers', by whom he meant Jack Fingleton and Bill O'Reilly. A batsman and lethal bowler respectively from the Bradman era, Fingleton was a prolific writer of cricket columns and books, and Bill O'Reilly reported cricket for years for the *Sydney Morning Herald*. Test all-rounder and long-time Australian selector Sam Loxton described Fingleton and O'Reilly as Bradman's greatest critics, who 'let their bias, jealousy and animosity rise to the surface in their writings'.

Robinson, the cricket writer for whom Bradman had most time, said Bradman's defenders tended to lean too far in the opposite direction, making him out to be a saint, which he was not. 'Nineteen times out of 20 – as he saw it, every time – what was best for Don Bradman was best for his side, a shared benefit, and fellow players were better off for it,' according to Robinson. 'The odd occasion lacking that ratio could not escape their notice.' Fingleton and O'Reilly were persistent in their derogation of Bradman but Bradman never publicly rebutted their attacks. When Rivett forwarded Fingleton's request to him for Rivett's assistance in getting his latest book reviewed, years of pent-up frustration at the chips and slights broke through.

Bradman wrote to Rivett that, honestly and without bias, Fingleton's letter reeked to him of jealousy, bigotry, envy and ego. Bradman thought it outrageous that Fingleton should ask Rivett to write a review. This was something of an overreaction on the part of Bradman, who went on that it was unsurprising Fingleton was not better known as a cricket writer in Australia at the time. He ridiculed Fingleton's comment that he wanted his 'cobbers' in Canberra to know about his new book, saying he was glad Fingleton has some cobbers there: he only knew, he said, of one Fingleton had left in the cricketing world and that, claimed Bradman, had to do with things in common other than cricket. He was presumably referring to Bill O'Reilly.

It was typical of Fingleton, Bradman went on, that he could be sarcastic about English cricket writer Jim Swanton in his letter to Rivett, while at the same time trying to curry favour with Swanton in his correspondence with him. He contrasted Fingleton's approach with Ray Robinson's 'suberb' review of Swanton's most recent book: 'Dear old Ray. Pity J.F. hadn't some of Ray's modesty.'

Rivett had asked Bradman whether he wanted to comment on Fingleton's statements about him personally. 'Well I would prefer not to even recognise Fingleton. He has spent virtually a lifetime of using me as a meal ticket for his own monetary reward and falsely attacking me by attributing to me attitudes which I did not possess. This latest is a perfect example. He knows full well that he can make that filthy accusation against me in that Perth game because nobody but me can dispute it. So it is one man's word against another's. It is just merely a lie – that's all. But what is the use of one making a comment that another man is telling a lie. I repeat that I prefer to ignore him. He is not worth recognising.'

When this letter was first reported in 2004, the Fingleton estate assumed it related to the long-running bodyline 'only one side is playing cricket' controversy since its location in Perth was not mentioned in the report. However, the 'filthy accusation' from 'that Perth game' appears to be a reference to an incident between Bradman and Fingleton in October 1932 when the Combined Australian XI played Jardine's MCC side in the run-up to the bodyline tests. Fingleton was relatively inexperienced at that stage, having made his test debut against South Africa in its 1931 tour of Australia.

Cricket writer David Frith recounts how Bradman, Fingleton and McCabe travelled five days by train from Sydney to reach Perth, with Richardson and Roy Lonergan joining them in Adelaide. Bradman was just twenty-four years old, and it was already as though a god was a passenger on the train. Word had got out and worshippers would move 'frantically along the platform or through the carriages, demanding The Don's acknowledgement of their adulation', Frith reports. Country towns on the route insisted on civic receptions. In Coolgardie goldminers stampeded, wanting to see and touch the great man, and when he locked himself in his cabin, they started to ransack the train. A police escort was needed to get Bradman and his fellow players to the Palace Hotel when the train arrived in Perth.

In the game, played at the WACA, Jardine saved Larwood and used fast bowler Gubby Allen to begin testing the Australian batsmen. Frith quotes Fingleton claiming in later years that during the Combined XI's second innings 'Bradman said to him in mid-pitch, 'I think they're going to have a pop at me', and requested him to take Allen's bowling.' Fingleton's slur was that, in effect, Bradman was a coward. Bradman was outraged.

Why would Fingleton make such an accusation? It was a particularly nasty sledge against one of his own team-mates that dovetailed into the hated Jardine's private declaration prior to the tour that 'he's yellow', based on viewing film of Bradman allegedly flinching at a Larwood delivery at The Oval in 1930. 'This conviction, although incorrect . . . gave Jardine and his men a confidence that had been lacking since the terrible summer of 1930,' according to Jardine biographer Christopher Douglas. He may or may not have flinched, but the figures speak for themselves: Bradman made 232 runs and effectively won the match for Australia.

Fingleton was the same age as Bradman. As a batsman he would always be in Bradman's shadow, as were all other good batsmen of that generation ever after. Fingleton's test average was 42.46 as against Bradman's 99.94. Fingleton was dropped for Australia's 1934 Ashes tour after a disappointing end to his otherwise gutsy performance in the bodyline series, and his friend Tiger O'Reilly said it scarred his later, much more cautious performances. (He subsequently made a successful comeback and notched up 18 Test matches in all.) Perhaps Victor Richardson, his *amour propre* offended by Bradman's edge over him for the South

Australian and Australian captaincies in the mid-1930s, coloured the young Fingleton's view of Bradman. Or perhaps journalist and author Jack Pollard's story of Fingleton training in the early years of World War II at the Paddington club's Trumper Park contains a clue to the psychology fuelling Fingleton's pursuit of Bradman.

Fingleton was playing grade cricket for Waverley at the time but could not get to Waverley Oval for practice. Paddington captain Mort Cohen invited him to train at Trumper Park where Paddington's bowlers loved the chance to roll a few up to the famous Test batsman. Pollard, observing one day, was stunned at Fingleton's extraordinary batting performance. He approached Billy Wells, Paddington's club president and also a state selector, and commented on Fingleton's brilliance. 'Billy was unimpressed,' Pollard reported. "The greatest practice wicket batsman Australia has ever had – but watch how he goes tomorrow in his match when things really count," said Wells. Sure enough reports of next day's grade matches carried accounts of Fingleton's slow batting against bowlers who should not have got a ball past him.' In other words, and in sharp contrast to Bradman whose on-field confidence and concentration were legendary, Fingleton had a temperament problem.

Fingleton himself attributed his animosity towards Bradman to the leaking of Australian captain Bill Woodfull's locker-room comments at the depths of the bodyline series. Woodfull told England tour manager 'Plum' Warner: 'There are two teams out there but only one of them is playing cricket.' The comment made its way into the press and the source was a mystery. Jardine biographer Christopher Douglas concluded that the source would never be known for sure: 'Bradman said it was Fingleton, Fingleton said it was Bradman and Leo O'Brien (the twelfth man) further confused the issue by revealing in an interview with *Wisden Cricket Monthly* that neither Bradman nor Fingleton was in the room at the time of the exchange, but Ryder and Kippax, who were both reporting the matches in one way or another, were.' Fingleton was out for a duck the next time he was at the wicket, bowled by Larwood, to whom Plum Warner had promised a reward should he get him out quickly: payback.

Fingleton blamed Bradman for not clearing his name over the leak. He claimed Bradman was the source and that journalist Claude Corbett, who got the story, told him so – but he levelled the accusation after Corbett was dead, making direct confirmation impossible. Cricket writer David Frith, in the most comprehensive account of the leak, cites journalist Gerald Mant, who also covered the bodyline series, as arguable corroboration for Fingleton's claim. Mant was told by Corbett's daughter that after Claude died her mother had said he had identified Bradman as the source of the leak. 'Claude Corbett was a down-to-earth, hard-drinking and convivial character, fond of a practical joke,' Mant said. 'Perhaps he had perpetrated a gigantic leg-pull on Fingleton but it was scarcely conceivable that he would do the same thing to his wife.'

All up the Corbett story is hearsay and could not be tested, and neither did Corbett's daughter hear the alleged disclosure first-hand. Journalists who disclose sources are by definition untrustworthy, and it is difficult to believe Corbett would have broken this cardinal rule of journalism and still retained professional standing and respect. Frith cites Mant pointing out that Leo O'Brien had spread the word on Woodfull's comments to the rest of the team and that any of them could have been the source. Frith wisely concludes that 'we have a choice as to which version we accept', and leaves it at that. In Frith's judgement whoever was responsible, the leak in fact served cricket well.

The trustees of Fingleton's estate fiercely assert the veracity of the Corbett story. They are on stronger ground, perhaps, disputing Bradman's allegation in his letter to Rohan Rivett that Fingleton had used Bradman as a meal ticket in his career as a journalist and author. After news of the Bradman letters to Rivett broke, trustee Malcolm Gemmell told the *Australian* that writing was Fingleton's livelihood and that he wrote professionally on sport and politics for outlets here and abroad. Moreover, it was impossible to write about twentieth century cricket and not write extensively about the player of the century.

Why were these old volcanic fights, which should have been extinct long before, still simmering? In a 1981 letter to Jardine's biographer, Christopher Douglas, Fingleton described a dream he had recently had about replaying a bodyline test, and the tactics he was going to use to better protect the off stump. '[Forty-eight] years on and still dreaming about it,' Douglas marvelled. The bodyline series never lost its grip.

So it was that Bradman's rage was fresh when he received Rivett's missive in February 1973. But it was Fingleton's accusation of cowardice during the Australian Combined XI match against MCC in the run-up to the bodyline tests that especially ignited his wrath. Frith's account of Fingleton's accusation bears further examination, that 'Bradman said to him in mid-pitch, "I think they're going to have a pop at me", and requested him to take Allen's bowling.'

Bodyline bowling *was* adopted by Jardine in England's 1932–33 Ashes tour expressly to contain Bradman: as a run-getter off the scale compared to other batsmen, he *was* the chief target, the player England needed to neutralise to win back the prize.

Secondly, bodyline bowling was terrifying; fast bowling is generally designed to intimidate, and bowling directly at the body exponentially so. But there is no evidence that Bradman any more than any other batsman in the bodyline series was intimidated by the English tactics. What was different was Bradman's response to the gauntlet thrown down by the English.

Typically, Bradman thought his way through the problem and devised what was in his view a more effective response than standing like a dumb ox taking a pounding in front of the stumps from Harold Larwood. Christopher Douglas describes how Bradman had toyed with the technique he devised at the Second Test in Melbourne, employing it fully in the rest of the series. As the ball charged towards him Bradman stepped back towards leg and hit it into the vacant off-side area, scoring runs at a rapid rate. Bradman was not one for pointless heroics: his job, as he saw it, was to make runs and avoid serious injury, and if the unorthodox method he employed worked best he was not about to let accusations that it lacked 'pluck' intimidate him into dropping it. Douglas describes its pivotal importance in, for example, bodyline's Fourth Test:

> The early dismissals of Fingleton and Ponsford were mortal blows to the Australian cause in the third innings of the fourth Test. Woodfull, and later on Richardson, played stubbornly, their pluck being duly recorded. But Bradman used his 'cut and run' method to score 66 in even time. It was an innings of sheer genius, but to some it looked suspiciously as if he wasn't trying, and Woodfull is said to have wanted to

> drop him from the side. The crowd loved it, though, and their excitement was further heightened by the extravagant ducking and weaving that the Australians had taken to – this practice was adopted in varying degrees throughout the rest of the series, much to the annoyance of the English bowlers.

Dancing about outside the leg stump, as Douglas describes it, worked a treat. While bodyline bowling succeeded in halving Bradman's batting average for the Test series, it remained in excess of 50 and he led the Australian batting average in the series by a considerable margin. As was so often the case in his career, Bradman was immune to peer pressure and found his own way to succeed irrespective of pack opinion.

Whether or not Rivett would agree to Fingleton's request to review the book for the *Canberra Times*, Bradman did not know. If Rivett were to be paid for it he may feel that he had to for professional reasons. But if it was voluntary he said he would be surprised if Rivett went ahead – not least because, given Rivett's own apparent view of Fingleton conveyed in the accompanying letter, he could end up in the libel courts over the piece.

The worst critics, said Bradman, were those with a 'fictitious reputation' who had never put anything back into the game and attacked those who did. He, Bradman, had spent much more time working voluntarily in cricket administration alone than Fingleton had spent as a player, and his conscience was clear that he had repaid his debt to the game. Could Fingleton, he posed, go to sleep happily at night with the same thought?

At the letter's end Bradman disclosed the reason *he* believed Fingleton waged a war against him: for 'exposing' him over

Bradman, 22 years old, answering mail on the 1930 Ashes Tour of England. His tendency to attend to correspondence and listen to classical music in the evenings rather than go out carousing jarred with some team mates early in his test career.

Rohan Rivett batting, aged six. Rivett was cricket mad throughout his life.

Bradman, then Australian captain, playing cricket with patients at the Perth Children's Hospital. His charitable activities continued until ill health and old age intervened.

Bradman spends an entire Sunday signing 3500 cricket bats destined to be sold in Australia and South Africa, June 1948. His readiness to sign bats, letters from admirers, provide autographs and so on undercut the scarcity value of his signature as a tradeable good.

Bradman relaxes at the home of English test cricketer Walter Robins in Berkshire, 1938, watched by Jessie (left) and Mrs Robins.

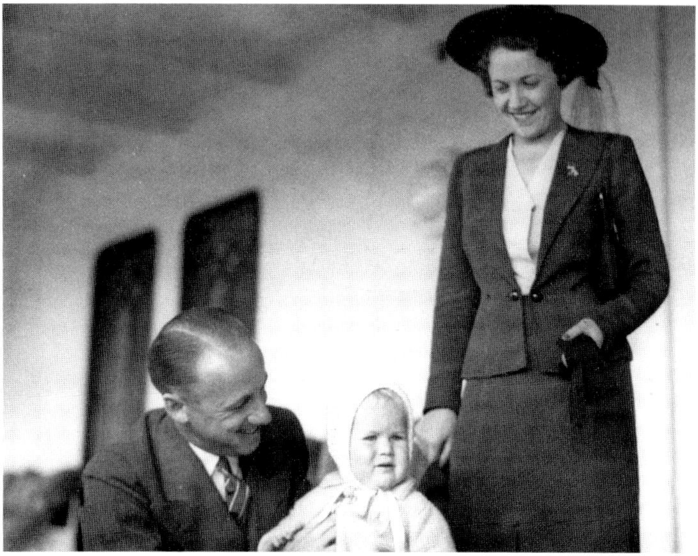

John's birth in 1939 was a joy to Don and Jessie, especially given the terrible loss of their first child shortly after birth.

John Bradman batting as a boy. Despite subsequent childhood polio, John displayed considerable cricket talent as a teenager and was an elite-level hurdler.

Bradman uses a blue silk handkerchief to test the breeze before England bats at the Fifth Test at The Oval, August 1948.

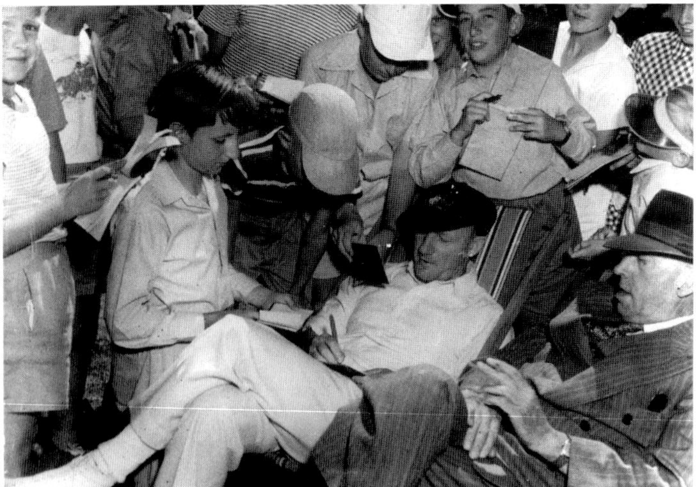

Bradman, 44, signs autographs at a non-competition game in Adelaide, February 1953.

Rohan Rivett at his desk as editor-in-chief of The News, *Adelaide.*

Rivett watches a game: he preferred the outer to the members' stand.

bodyline. Bradman outlined how in his 1950 book *Farewell to Cricket* he had mentioned the bitter criticism he had endured over his particular tactics for dealing with bodyline bowling. He singled out Fingleton for mention as a contemporary player and then commentator who had cast 'grave reflections' on his tactics.

Bradman told Rivett that he had then reminded readers that Fingleton's last three Test innings in the bodyline series saw him score a single and two ducks, at which point Fingleton was dropped from the team. In contrast, in the same three innings and facing the same bowling onslaught, Bradman had scored 277 at an average of 88.5 – figures which rather pulled the rug out from under Fingleton's criticism. 'Jack has never forgiven me for that,' Bradman told Rivett. 'The truth really hurt.'

Bradman's private square-up with Fingleton in the security of his correspondence with Rivett was done. He moved onto the current struggle: the Ian Chappell-led Australian tour of the West Indies in 1972–73. From that distance the contest seemed interesting but not quite top level.

In March 1973 Bradman wrote that lightening his cricket administration load somewhat had made things a bit easier for him on the health front. Though rarely moving outside Adelaide that season, he said he had enjoyed the cricket, especially the Pakistanis earlier in the summer: 'fresh and interesting & there was some excellent play'. The West Indies tour was then looking more doubtful. Massie and Lillee both being out was a surprise, he thought. Massie had suddenly lost the ability to swing the ball, and Lillee had a serious back injury.

A few months later, in July 1973, Bradman announced his

retirement as president of the South Australian Cricket Association, effective from September. But as the 1970s wore on, Bradman's involvement and concern with national cricket administration intensified. Any idea he entertained of easing himself out of his responsibilities as an Australian administrator was dashed as the old cricket ways began to unravel.

A plethora of umpire reports concerning foul language and unsporting behaviour on the field in first class matches triggered a letter from the Board of Control to all state cricket associations that year. Player unrest and dissatisfaction with pay levels were growing. Ian Chappell locates the origins of Kerry Packer's World Series Cricket in the poor pay and conditions and antediluvian rules facing cricketers in the 1970s. Chappell's own repeated efforts to make representations to the Board of Control failed. Bradman had generally been a force for progress on the board; as a young player he had had several notable run-ins himself with it over conditions and constraints placed on him as a test cricketer. But when it came to money, Bradman had a blind spot and Chappell found him particularly unresponsive on what was, at its essence, the key issue propelling cricketers into the waiting arms of Kerry Packer.

There was symmetry in the fact that it was Victor Richardson's grandson who led the charge into cricket's modern media era. 'Ian, a rebel in his youth, was a superb leader of men in his prime and a deep thinker and writer on the game with the mellowing of middle age,' Chris Harte has written of Chappell. 'His family's feud with Bradman has lasted to this day with the clash of iron wills and personalities [helping] cause the eruptions of later years.'

In October 1976 Bradman told Rivett he had noticed how

busy he had been with various press, radio and television engagements – and that Rivett had made friendly mention of Bradman's friend Tony Charlton, who had recently visited Adelaide for a function. It was an award presentation for Ian Chappell 'so on principle I refused to attend – my mute protest at his approach to life'.

Ray Robinson, on the other hand, came in for mutual approbation from the two men. Rivett had written in praise of Robinson, but saying he got too little credit for his great cricket reportage. Bradman agreed with his estimation of Robinson but said that in 'my circles at least he is tops, and everyone says so, and I certainly give him credit at every opportunity'. Bradman thought his praise for Robinson's book *On Top Down Under* had helped it achieve a second edition, with the bonus that its numerous errors could be corrected.

Behaviour standards were playing on Bradman's mind: 'I still hope to see us get rid of players who abuse umpires and defile the standards of cricket – even though in the short term they can line their pockets.' But he felt personally content with his cricketing existence: he had been lucky to have played or administered cricket for half the whole history of test matches, he told Rivett. His peaceful satisfaction, however, was about to be shattered by Kerry Packer.

But not before another Bradman–Rivett exchange on selection. Rivett's picks were unlikely to be smiled on officially – not that the official selection would do any better than Rivett's pick. As to Rivett's crack that Bradman favoured Sam Loxton's judgement when it came to selection, Bradman demurred and claimed he had never said anything good, bad or indifferent about Loxton's judgement. 'Nor do I influence him,' quipped Bradman. 'He goes his own way in cricket matters as with wives.'

Rivett wrote to Bradman in March 1977, prompted by reading a piece Bradman had written about the future of cricket in the *Centenary Cricket Magazine*. 'I suspect we will end up with artificial pitches, weatherproof stadiums, fluorescent lighting when needed, and all top players jetting from Test match to Test match – perhaps 15 or 20 each calendar year,' Rohan wrote. Neither man knew just how close such things were.

The last substantial cricket exchange between the two came just as Kerry Packer's move on Australian cricket was gaining momentum. Rivett wrote, in Bradman's view valiantly, in support of traditional cricket. Bradman was all the more touched because Rivett had often been critical of the existing cricket administration.

It was early days, Bradman told Rivett, but he was convinced – wrongly – that 'Packer's circus will fail'. Even if that was the upshot, however, he thought enormous damage would be done to the existing structures supporting the game. 'It is a pity that the whole truth of how well the players are doing cannot be told,' Bradman wrote. 'One is not privy to the knowledge of the taxation commissioner but the stars like Lillee & co (who cry poor mouth) have undoubtedly been making enormous money by any standards.'

Bradman suggested to Rivett that he might want to take influential administrator Bob Parish to lunch some time, to get more information about the struggle. The media, fearing writs, was apparently reluctant to cross Packer with critical articles, Bradman observed, but he speculated that Rivett 'may be exempt' from such strictures. His friend did not live long enough to report much further on developments, or see the struggle played out.

Arguably, the jury is still out on whether the modern media

takeover of the game has resulted in 'too much cricket', which Bradman identified in the 1960s as a factor tending to breed 'an air of contempt' in the media towards cricket, if not among followers of the game. Signs of follower fatigue have appeared among fans of tennis, which has generally been a few years ahead of cricket in the media appropriation and expansion curve: the plethora of tournaments has overwhelmed and partly obscured the pleasurable ebb and flow of the traditional tennis timetable. It is too early to tell whether cricket will suffer the same fate.

3 *Investment*

'Should I sell News yet?'

— Don Bradman

Bradman's approach to investment was meticulous, value-oriented and sceptical of speculative plays. Many of the letters to Rivett contain lengthy commentaries on his friend's diverse share portfolio, at Rivett's urging. In the other direction Bradman would defer to Rivett's expert knowledge and insider perspective in relation to media shares though, as the correspondence shows, such knowledge was naturally not enough to guarantee that Rivett always called media shares the right way.

Australian resource stock AOG was the first investment issue to arise in the correspondence preserved in the Rivett Papers. In a letter to Rivett in April 1962 Bradman describes without comment AOG's share price volatility. The shares had fallen 20 shillings on an announcement of no oil at 5795 feet in 'No 3 well' one day, and risen 26 shillings the next day on the announcement of 1500 barrels a day at 5800 feet in the same well. Rivett, by now working as chief of the International Press Institute in Zurich, was voracious for news of the Australian markets and Bradman kept him well supplied with news of announcements and anecdotes of this kind.

Easter 1962 saw News Limited steady at 14s 3d, Bradman relayed to Rivett, Queensland Press 'strong' on 70 shillings and announcing a new issue along with Burns Philp and CSR, but the market overall he judged not very active.

Bradman was concerned about the uncertain outlook and felt somewhat pessimistic. In June 1962 he noted the Philippines claim on North Borneo, Soekarno sending more troops into what Bradman called New Guinea (part of Indonesia's bid for what would become Irian Jaya) and South Australian establishment luminary Sir Lloyd Dumas fighting with the Adelaide Stock Exchange – all in one sentence. The world had never seemed more topsy-turvy, he confided to his friend. The market pointed to a depression in his view, but some analysts had forecast a boom: 'Who is right?'

Whitegoods maker Pope was struggling as the impact of the 1961 credit squeeze worked its way through the economy. 'I see no early return to prosperity here because, even when turnovers are restored, profitability is reduced,' Bradman wrote in the harbinger of what was to be an enduring theme about the prospects for business generally.

Writing from Switzerland, in July 1962, prior to a visit home to Australia later that year, Rivett asked Bradman to review his portfolio of forty-two stocks. He would not trade further until talking to Bradman on that visit, he said. 'My main comment on your list,' replied Bradman, 'is that I wish it was mine.' He had reservations about a couple of stocks but thought Rivett should leave his generally fine portfolio alone, pending any sign of an improving market.

He did advise Rivett to check which share registers his stocks were held on given the significant difference it could make to estate taxes. 'We never know what the future holds and neglect of this simple precaution of putting your holdings on the best register can, in certain circumstances, be very costly,' Bradman wrote. Woolworths was an example where, if held on the Canberra register instead of the Sydney register, a great deal of 'inconvenience and cost' could be saved.

The following year, 1963, saw a flurry of correspondence largely dedicated to Rivett's share portfolio and trades made on it through Bradman. Rivett wrote to Bradman in May about purchasing shares. Bradman wrote back quickly and set out planned purchases of shares for him including BHP, CSR, Feltex (rights), Edment's, Herald's, James Hardie and Malcolm Moore. The stocks and the size of the purchase had been finalised after consulting his stockbroking colleague Don Hackett, and the orders had been placed through the firm of his friend Len Bullock.

On the other side of the slate, Bradman told Rivett to avoid television stocks: 'Television will lose money for some time and my information is that T.V. companies are finding things much tougher.' He continued to be down on Ansett shares, a view expressed in earlier letters, and argued that in any case there would be better buying opportunities for the stock, especially if the then opposition leader, Arthur Calwell, won the next election. Rivett's interest in Latec was not shared, and nor did Bradman support his friend's enthusiasm for hotel stocks like Federal Hotels; as a class he believed they were getting hit hard by competition from motels. 'Federals do look reasonable at 3/9 but I scent difficulties ahead,' Bradman wrote.

The investment side of the correspondence shows Bradman

keenly engaged in the equities market, his knowledge detailed and up to date – so up to date that in one particular letter he moves from sending his love to Rivett's wife Nan in the closing paragraph to: 'Oh – just saw it. Can't tell you why N.T. have gone up. Don't know.' He must have been watching the ticker as he typed.

There is further evidence of a meticulous, professional approach to investment, including its interaction with the tax system – awareness and knowledge highly valued by high net worth investors. He advised Rivett in May 1963, for example, to hold off acquiring Ampol and, instead, to buy rights to the new deferred shares about to be released: 'You will [thus] acquire equity at the best possible price, with deferred income and saving of tax. I reckon you'll get them this way for less than 6/– with no dividends for 4 years – a better bargain.' Bradman said he hoped Rivett agreed with the decisions made by him with Don Hackett after their long conversation about Rivett's financial affairs.

But there had been a serious misunderstanding about the share purchases. Bradman's next letter portrays Rivett as fickle and prone to wrong-headedly stubborn behaviour. 'As usual your letter leaves me completely mystified and, having read it to DLH,' Bradman said, drawing Don Hackett into the fray on his side of the disagreement, 'both of us are now mystified.' Rivett was again on the road, this time in Sweden, where the letter was sent care of Stockholm's K.A.K. Hotel.

Bradman said their understanding had been that Rivett wanted some three thousand pounds worth of shares, and they had bought accordingly. They further understood that Rivett then wanted to buy notes and debentures. But Rivett's latest letter had left them confused, to put it politely, about whether he wanted to buy further shares first or go ahead with the notes and debenture purchases. In any case, Bradman swatted, according to Hackett 'you haven't anything like the amount to invest which you have been talking about'. Stock by stock Bradman then gives an unadorned view of the companies raised by Rivett in his latest letter.

Rivett might be right about Latec, Bradman said, but it was impossible to confirm the value of the firm's physical assets. Reflecting the true instincts of a value investor, Bradman told Rivett he would not risk the purchase on his own initiative. Turning to Myer he agreed the retailer had prospects, but said it would need to have: 'It is I think the lowest yield of any Australian share.' Rivett would be wasting money buying Herald & Weekly Times options when the shares represented better value. He again spelled out why buying rights to the new deferred shares issued by Ampol would be better than buying Ampol shares.

Generally one to favour retailers, Bradman said he agreed that Woolworths, Coles and John Martins were all good, despite low yields, for long term growth. Rivett, he implied, had confused Western Titanium and N.W. Tantalum to come up with the non-existent N.W. Titanium. But rather than rubbing it in he enclosed a newspaper cutting on Western Titanium. He did not hold back, however, in relation to Federal Hotels: 'So you want to buy because Shaul is the best manager in the business. One of the reasons I suggested not buying was that Shaul has just resigned. Not only that but John O'Neill (Chairman City Mutual) whom I know extremely well and who is a most capable chap, has also resigned.' Rivett's comments on the company's assets were correct and there was a possibility the price could pick up, Bradman conceded, 'but I dislike shows where there is trouble in the air'. Nor did he like hotels as an investment class at that time, he reiterated from the previous correspondence.

The letter's barely restrained hectoring is briefly unleashed over brokerage rates. Bradman told Rivett that his 'dig' about Bullock's brokerage rates had been noted: 'May I just repeat what I understand you have been told 3 times already, namely that Adelaide & Melbourne rates ARE NOW THE SAME.' He and Hackett had decided to make no further move pending clarification of Rivett's plans. The normally warm closing remarks of love for Nan and the family are confined to a crisp: 'Hope all well.' There are only a couple of letters in the long correspondence in this tone, but they show Bradman at his most brusque and, almost, bruising when he felt piqued over a matter of substance.

There is a gap of several weeks judging by the letters preserved after this strained exchange. But the next in the series – from Bradman to Rivett, who was back in Zurich, in July 1963 – showed them as intimately engaged in investment matters as ever they had been, and again on friendly personal terms.

The letter is a perfect expression of Bradman the broker. The advice is detailed. It is sound both tactically and strategically, prudent without being defensive. It is based on a comprehensive yet concise appreciation of the swing factors for each stock or class canvassed, both in terms of the corporate and political factors which could impact on price.

In one typed, single-spaced aerogram page Bradman comments on two dozen stocks, canvasses the impact of relevant Indonesian and US government policy, outlines near term macroeconomic scenarios in Australia, agitates against 'odds' – small, odd-sized parcels of shares – and advises Rivett to establish an over policy for his portfolio as a prelude to some rationalisation. Rivett owned so many different stocks, he said, that the portfolio in its current state really required daily attention. It needed pruning.

It was 'lunacy' to hold onto odd lots like Rivett's George Wardrop preferences shares. They should go in a general tidying of the portfolio. 'It seldom pays to chase bad stocks,' Bradman told his friend, 'and it is mostly better to cut a loss and make it up on a good stock.'

Bradman encouraged Rivett to look at his portfolio in a more integrated way when making decisions about individual stocks. Why decide to sell Howard Smith but hold BHP, for example, when Howard Smith owned so many shares in BHP? Rivett should look to realise the value in fully optimised stocks and trade in those shares on others with better prospects. Stocks like Argo were unlikely to bring Rivett much more joy: 'Safe and solid but a switch to say A.P.M. would surely offer better prospects both for capital and yield.'

Bradman challenged Rivett's possibly jaundiced view of the holding company of his old competitor from Adelaide newspaper days, the city's morning daily, the *Advertiser*. 'At the outset I cringed at your reference to Advertisers as a 2nd class stock, especially when Sir Lloyd is in Melbourne gallantly fighting a lone hand against a 3rd T.V. Station,' Bradman wrote. The firm not only owned Adelaide's morning daily paper but also an interest in one of the city's then two commercial television stations, Channel 7. The other station was owned by PBL, Sir Frank Packer's family company. Bradman saw in a heroic light the futile fight of ultimate Adelaide insider, Sir Lloyd Dumas, to stop the issuing of a third television licence which would eat into the two existing licensees' broadcast advertising revenue. Bradman advised him to hold his *Advertiser* shares. Rupert Murdoch subsequently won the struggle, emerging with the third licence for Channel 10, complementing his afternoon daily, the *News*.

Rivett was grateful for Bradman's advice. It had already generated two letters to Don Hackett, he said in a reply from Zurich in August 1963, and possible trades through Bullock and Co if Hackett had passed the content of those missives on. Rivett asked forgiveness for a further 'infliction', as he put his plea for more advice. Rivett summed his portfolio up thus: around twenty-seven stocks, of which twenty were blue chip, worth in total fifty thousand pounds, plus another seventy lesser stocks worth in total twenty thousand pounds, with the total portfolio worth a considerable seventy thousand pounds. Rivett had taken a haircut in the credit squeeze engineered by the Menzies Government in 1961. Now, two years later and about to repatriate to Australia, Rivett told Bradman that financial security was at a premium for him and his family in the coming year. 'But I've never yet found how you get out at the very top and as a layman, right out of touch over here until December when I get home, I'd rather not be sick and sorry again and [find] next March that what is worth over £50,000 now is worth less than £40,000 then,' he told Bradman. 'And that's just what happened to lots of us – and worse – three months after Holt and Ming did their little piece in November, 1961.'

The alternative scenario Rivett put to Bradman was to do nothing with the portfolio – to take a calculated risk on the assumption that Menzies would not run a deflationary economic policy in the run-up to an election. Rivett the political analyst rated this slightly more likely than not – a 51/49 chance. But

Rivett the investor had a strong preference not to get burned again. He would be a 'bloody sight unhappier', he wrote, if he did nothing and the stockmarket then fell than if he reweighted his portfolio to include more fixed interest and share prices did not fall.

A middle course was counselled by Bradman, who seemed pleased Rivett was taking his investment advice seriously. He singled out Rivett's sale, on the basis of a Bradman hint, of one stock at 77 shillings which fell the next week on the announcement of a heavy profit drop to 67 shillings. 'One can be so wrong,' wrote Bradman, 'but occasionally one "knows".' Conditions were 'set fair' for good share prices in the near term, in his view, and newspapers were among the best of the picks. He agreed with Rivett that they were selling at a premium – and why not, asked Bradman, given the commanding position and, in that pre-internet era, inbuilt security?

Another of Bradman's investment rules of thumb emerged wittily in this letter, triggered by Rivett's enthusiasm for the firm Nappie Wash. 'I just hate unlisted stocks and don't know anything about that company,' he wrote. 'I'll leave that baby to you.' He again urged Rivett to focus on the net effect of any moves to change the relative weighting of equities and fixed interest in his portfolio. After transaction costs and tax were taken into account, the numbers were much less attractive than on first blush. There was also a chance, warned Bradman, that too much activity could lead the Commissioner of Taxation to classify Rivett as a trader, resulting in tax on Rivett's capital profits. 'The man who never sells a share (providing his selection is right) probably does as well or better than the man who buys and sells to try and catch the ups and downs,' Bradman wrote. 'In the end probate gets most of it anyway.'

The death of his old friend and stockbroking colleague Len Bullock in February 1964 stalled Bradman's appetite for chewing over stocks with Rivett. But things were resolved in March and the intense investment dialogue then resumed. The market was high, Bradman observed, going on typically to question how long that could last. He was mystified by what News was up to in New Zealand and reported that, despite the negative information about the *Advertiser* Rivett had reported to Bob Pentelow, the stock looked firm. Unlike Rivett, Bradman said he could not get excited about N.W. Tantalum and its manoeuvres in relation to Placer N.L. It all looked like a gamble to Bradman. 'If the tin price holds maybe the show will succeed,' he wrote. 'If not where are the assets?'

By May health woes for both men had stemmed the investment chat. Bradman told Rivett he had been right about the price of News weakening. Bradman subsequently stirred Rivett up about his later media stock calls. Nostalgically he dug out his old 'Don Bradman & Co.' letterhead from the days he had his own firm and wrote to Rivett. He was trying to evoke happier days after following Rivett's advice that Bradman should buy Syme shares, which had then gone down, and to sell News shares, which had then gone up.

The Hamersley Iron float covering huge ore reserves in Western Australia intrigued Bradman because of its sheer size, audacity, extraordinary profit projections and lack of income for the first several years of the project. He mused about whether investor enthusiasm could be maintained for that long without income. If the opportunity to take up some Hamersley shares came by he wrote that he would most likely 'join the mob' and do so, to take a quick profit if it was there. Yet Bradman said he had more faith in BHP due to the likely returns from its oil and gas finds over the same period.

Modestly, Bradman told Rivett that he was really not in a position to judge the Hamersley venture. But he did manage to score a point over Rivett's gloom on monetary policy. 'As my name is not Nugget (Coombs – not Miller), and my degrees in economics nil, far be it from me to question your judgement,' Bradman wrote of Rivett's dismissal of any prospect for an interest rate cut. But he went on to draw his friend's attention to a newspaper cutting he enclosed reporting the Bank of England's second interest rate cut in a year, with a consequential boost in British share prices. Yes, it was Britain, not Australia, he conceded: 'But can Australia isolate herself from the world *for long*, on any matter including interest rates? I doubt that she can.'

Bradman expressed fears for Australian share prices, not from any threat of higher interest rates but because business was being 'bled white' by having to absorb big cost increases while facing 'extreme competition'. How could companies stay in the black, he wanted to know, when faced by compulsory unionism, equal pay for women, price controls and restrictive trade practices legislation? Bradman forecast somewhat faster economic growth accompanied by rising inflation and a certain decline in the Australian dollar. This all left the 'poor old investor' in a quandary about whether to go for assured income or tangible assets. 'My money is still to have a bit both ways,' he declared.

Wage increases not easily absorbed by small players were a major worry to Bradman. 'Our Lords & Masters' had handed down a basic wage increase of one pound a week – easy for the Myers and Woolworths of the world to pay for, but a struggle for firms already finding it tough to make profits, he argued.

In September 1964 Bradman again evaluated Rivett's portfolio in some detail, along with a follow-up on Rivett's subsequent comments. Bradman said it was not a market in which one's luck should be trusted too far, and that a reasonable stake in fixed interest securities would be wise.

Quality of management emerged as a key factor in Bradman's company evaluations. Bradman told Rivett he was biased against one particular company because 'management is their big problem'. Conversely, he favoured Swift's despite their disappointing performance: Bradman approved of the 'good and sound' chairman, Ron Irish, and felt the firm would do better. Some of Rivett's investments puzzled Bradman. The uranium stock Kathleen Investments was 'a bit of a mystery' to him. 'A sudden break through in the usage of atomic power and they would be booming again,' he supposed. 'I should say that is more likely to happen than that Timors will strike oil.'

Bradman tried to get Rivett to accept the idea of sunk costs – money that had been lost and could not be recovered – when working out whether to sell off one stock in favour of another. Rivett's 28 per cent book loss on a particular stock was immaterial to that decision, he argued: 'That has happened. It is factual. The only justification for holding would be the belief that this stock offers better prospects of a rise *from now* than anything else.'

Interest in shares was waning for Bradman, and this may have been bound up in his relative pessimism about the outlook. The market was 'dangerously high', in his view, and there was money to be made selling out one's portfolio and staying out of the market altogether for a year. The trouble was that money was losing its value so fast. As he became more pessimistic, the premium he put on a company having sound management grew. Even as Bradman's interest in the market declined, however, there was one enterprise he was, and remained, curious about. It was the future of Rupert Murdoch's new national daily newspaper, the *Australian* and its likely impact on News Limited: 'I confess to wondering how the *Australian* can ever hope to earn a profit.' It was a puzzle to which he would return again and again with Rivett, Murdoch's former friend and colleague.

Rivett offered a scenario. Bradman remained sceptical. 'If Rupert can't step up his advertising over what I saw in one issue, he'll send News broke. Pity. I thought it a good paper but the concept ahead of its time.'

In the run-up to the 1964 half Senate election, Rivett again peppered Bradman with queries about potential share trades. Neither Olympics nor Dunlop appealed much, though he thought the latter a shade better; in Bradman's view competition in the rubber sector was set to intensify. Clifton Bricks might be all right in the short term, but he also forecast tougher competition in the market for bricks. He agreed with Rivett that resource stock Norths looked good, and that fertilisers had lost their appeal: 'Will the subsidy be repeated?' As for Ansett, he was still no fan but said the company was better placed then than ever before. The Menzies Government would still control 'the Reps' for another two years, even if Arthur Calwell's Labor Opposition won the half Senate election on the following Saturday. But Bradman's dubiousness about the market ran deep: 'Altogether why enter this market at all yet?' And still the effect of the *Australian* on the future of Rupert Murdoch's News Corporation continued to fascinate. Did Rivett think News could keep carrying its losses on the *Australian*?

Bradman maintained a professional manner and tone in his market commentaries, rarely betraying much ego. Flashes of professional pride were rare. One came in January 1965 over relative price movements between two pulp and paper companies, Associated Pulp and APM. Bradman had been waiting for weeks and weeks, he told Rivett, to see whether his advice, including specifics on price, would prove right. He couldn't resist pointing out that, to his satisfaction, he had not misled his friend. The predictions had been spot on.

March 1965 saw Bradman recommending 'recovery stocks' like Yarra Falls. Recovery stocks could be good buys, he argued, providing one picked well: 'A nice market rise is much better than a reasonable dividend.' Other stocks like Harris Scarfes, Clarksons and Thompson & Harvey looked cheaper, he said, but the market was not warming to them, perhaps through dread of the federal budget due in August and the prospect of higher interest rates. Bradman agreed with Rivett that Western Mining Company looked good, but said there was no hurry since, unless gold was revalued, the company's future lay in iron ore and aluminium, which both took time. South's was perhaps worth a look in the nearer term, he mused, given its copper prospects.

The 1965 UK budget alarmed Bradman, and combined with the interest rate outlook he saw little likelihood from his vantage point that April to suggest that Australian share prices would be on the rise.

Renison, which Rivett raised with him around this time, was a possible exception. Bradman thought the prospects for tin prices were good. Malaya was a big tin producer, he replied to his friend, and the area was likely to remain politically unstable for some time. There seemed to be something of a shortage of the metal, too, and at the time it was not reusable. If Renison's reserves and the economics of the project were sound, Bradman backed a 'flutter' on the stock. His only caveat was that some 'put' options had been written on them, which he thought not a good sign. Subsequently he cooled off on Renison which, ultimately, he decided was too speculative.

Rivett had been right about News, however, and Bradman continued to be fascinated by Murdoch's expansionary media highwire act: 'But surely the moment of truth is dawning and with all the inherent advantages and assets they must soon be good buying on the prospect of cutting losses and getting back to sanity.'

Overall Bradman's view of the market remained sober. Several factors were holding back prices. These included the Vietnam War, 'the impact of which is only now beginning to dawn on most Australians'; the drought; lower commodity export prices; weaker investment flows into Australia from the US and Britain; and budget measures likely to come as a result of those weaker flows of foreign investment dollars. A few specific individual company disasters had also shaken confidence in his view: 'I am tempted to say there is little to encourage investment before the budget.'

As 1965 continued, Bradman told Rivett that his attitude to the market had not changed: business was generally finding it harder every day to be profitable. There were many reasons, he thought, for maintaining a certain level of liquidity in that climate, looking to short term fixed interest assets with good yields. Though there were exceptions, he said: Bank of NSW, for example, which was good buying at 58 shillings with its 150th anniversary coming up the next year. Did Rivett have any Kelvinator shares in his portfolio, Bradman wanted to know?

Like any good stockbroker, Bradman combed his contacts for information about the ongoing performance of companies and significant developments affecting them. In September 1965 Bradman wrote to Rivett concerning a special client who owned a big parcel of News shares and had heard dismal things about the company's then state. Some months earlier Bradman had advised the client to reduce his holding of News somewhat on grounds that the *Australian* might drag its overall performance down. Now the client was thinking of quitting the stock altogether but had agreed to stay any action pending Bradman's intelligence gathering.

Bradman wanted Rivett's view. He guessed the *News* was doing all right in Adelaide and that most of the company's other ventures were okay. But was the *Australian* picking up or still losing sizable sums? 'If the latter,' he asked, 'will Rupert go on carrying the baby or will he close it up and call the venture a day?' What would Rivett do if facing this investment decision? He apologised for worrying his friend with these questions but said Rivett may have some up-to-date news affecting the decision, and that he would value his opinion.

Rivett wrote straight back: the letter arrived almost simultaneously with News' annual result. Rivett's analysis had been apt, Bradman wrote. The special client, who had been alarmed by the situation portrayed by some internal News staff, only sold a smallish percentage of his News shares as a result.

Bradman had something of a fascination with Murdoch, especially his massive taste for risk. He chewed over the future of the

Australian, and whether its losses would drag News down, like a dog worrying a bone: this was the single business question most often raised by Bradman in his long correspondence with Rivett. Bradman had been an aggressive, expansive batsman but with each shot calculated to the nth degree. Murdoch was an aggressive, expansionist businessman but Bradman sensed, perhaps, that Murdoch did not pin down the risk curve on each of his daring business strokes to the same extent. He thought it would be interesting to know how much of Murdoch's new venture had been capitalised versus written off: 'I see Rupert has camouflaged the position somewhat by his statement . . .' Why, the aging Bradman wanted to know, did some people with magnificent businesses risk them to achieve something which was 'not necessary anyhow'? It was a question unlikely to have occurred to him during his prime as a batsman, at the same age as the tyro media tycoon.

That same month, September 1965, saw a heavy fall in the Australian stockmarket. 'Of one thing I'm sure – I am more philosophic and worry far less than of yore about events wherein I can exercise no influence whatever,' Bradman wrote Rivett. But what matter if one did not have to sell and if income remained satisfactory? 'One tends to think more in *net* terms,' he said. In that environment Bradman leaned to blue chip stocks with considerable liquidity, like Woolworths, that were bound to pick up as the market revived. This was preferable to high yield 'semi-speculative, non-marketable' stocks, he argued. He told Rivett the market index could fall further but that several individual stocks – again he singled out Woolworths – were bottoming out.

But against the backdrop of inflation, holding cash or liquid short term investments was only worthwhile tactically with the aim of re-entering the market at the right time, Bradman argued. Otherwise lower purchasing power was inevitable as inflation ate away at the value of the liquid assets. Despite the possible fluctuations still on the way, rights in CSR, BHP, Woolworths and Bank of NSW all looked good to Bradman.

Bradman favoured Woolworths because, along with Coles, it was then 'delightfully free' from bad debts, problems related to Australia's impending conversion to decimal currency and from the Restrictive Trade Practices Bill: 'The latter hasn't grown any teeth yet but in other hands it will have molars. And certain people like ACI may well find it prudent *not* to do certain things just to play safe.' Bradman then workshopped the application of the trade practices legislation to the tyre manufacturers and whether they would quote identical prices on tyres to GMH once the Bill became law.

Cannily he focused, too, on the operation of South Australia's two cement companies. 'To buy cement you must go to a separate sales company, jointly owned by them, and the price is fixed,' he told Rivett. 'This is so obviously collusion that the winding up of the sales company would not surprise. And even then a verbal understanding on prices may be unlawful.' Cement companies subsequently attracted decades of intense interest from Australia's competition regulator, generating several significant court decisions penalising cement companies for collusion.

In this climate he doubted whether the existing yields of stocks subject to pressure from any crackdown on restrictive trade practices were adequate. Bradman said he would rather put his faith in stocks like the Bank of NSW 'which my grapevine tells me must be held'. It was far preferable to a stock with limited prospects like the Bank of Adelaide, for example, except for the latter's likelihood as a takeover target. A takeover had been in train, Bradman confided to Rivett, reaching an advanced stage when 'your great friend on North Terrace' – that is, Premier Tom Playford – intervened. Parochial state interests might make Playford's successors maintain a similar stance, he said: Rivett ought to switch out of Bank of Adelaide and into Bank of NSW.

Rivett continued keeping Bradman up to date with news on News. In October 1965 he flagged Murdoch's impending divorce from his first wife, Patricia. Bradman said he had not heard word of it but that, when it came to News' finances, 'I had worked out the story much as you unfolded it'. Bradman said he was amazed by men who put power and glory before all else. 'I marvel also at Directors who are prepared to stand pat on their legal as distinct from moral obligations to honour the debts of their wholly owned subsidiaries,' he wrote. 'What of the debenture holders who bought Palmers because they believed MLC would not let them down? It's a strange world.'

Bradman told Rivett he had just come from a Rotary Club lunch where Alf Gard had spoken in favour of a lottery for South Australia and Reverend Frank Seaman had spoken against. There was a sensation when Gard told the assembled businessmen to face up to the fact that many of them wouldn't have been there that day if someone hadn't gambled and lost: 'Some of the old boys were not amused.'

Even a seat on the Stock Exchange was no sure store of value in the 1960s. 'I see Hopman's seat brought $17,000,' he wrote to Rivett in April 1966. 'That is $8,000 below the peak if my memory is right.'

Later that year the investment banter picked up pace again. With exceptions, Bradman remained somewhat bearish. He wrote that Rivett's faith in 'Isa' (MIM) had been partly borne out with good results, and that the McArthur River find was bigger even than the Mt Isa resource itself: 'I expect they will have to cough up a very much more substantial slice of the cake to unions in the future but long range they look good.' Waltons also looked sounder, he thought. But overall, with costs rising and some strains evident in the world financial system, Bradman saw no bonanzas looming unless suddenly 'they lift gold to £10 an oz. & notes become worthless'.

The older he got, the less inclined Bradman was to forecast very far into the future. 'It seems to me we have to play it from day to day almost,' he told Rivett in August 1966. For some time, Bradman said, he had tended to play it safe, emphasising quality fixed interest assets like BHP debentures, and proven equities like Coles, Woolworths, Queensland Insurance, and Bankers and Traders. While 'gambling' on future metals prices was dangerous, EZ looked reasonable, too, he thought. Not so banks, which Bradman thought mostly had poor short term prospects, partly because of mounting wages bills, and motel stocks which he told Rivett to sell. There ought to be a place for transport stocks in his portfolio and the better ones would perform well, he said, but on the other hand it was a sector that would 'never get any help from any type of Government'. Government determination to take care of the railways would ensure that no bonanza from road transport investments would occur, he argued.

'No Rohan, I can't see any reason why the market as a whole should advance in the near future,' he wrote in August 1966. There would be individual company winners, but in a year's time he thought profits overall would be down. Fixed interest was his choice for the prevailing climate.

Bradman again gave a detailed analysis of several stocks for Rivett: some two and a half closely typed pages on eight separate stocks. His analysis of one, Olympic Consolidated Industries, showed his great grasp of business practicalities. The tyre-makers had just stepped back from a price war and put up prices five per cent – 'the first step back onto a profitable road', he told Rivett. However, there was massive excess capacity in Australian tyre production and a Firestone takeover of Hardie's was imminent, bringing another big American competitor into the market. But Bradman understood the importance of sales channels to profitability. 'Despite all this, Olympics are fairly well placed because of the tyre outlets which they secured when money had a greater value, and it is sales to the public which produce profit, not sales to General Motors etc,' he said. Bradman contrasted this with the situation of SA Rubber which had virtually no sales outlets.

Glass packaging company ACI should be in everyone's portfolio, he told Rivett. They were relatively impervious to competition except possibly from plastics – but ACI also had significant capacity there. Coles and Woolworths, too, Bradman continued to push: 'They are both miles below traditional values, and the present yields are almost unheard of.' Of Syme, the owner of the *Age* newspaper in Melbourne, Bradman said it would be ludicrous for him to advise when Rivett was in a much better position to tell. The yield was ridiculously poor, in Bradman's view, 'but the important factor is what goes on behind the scenes, rather than what appears on the surface'.

Bradman liked Pyrox. While the share price fluctuated, it was selling at 26 cents with a net asset backing of 60 cents and the board had foreshadowed a significant profit boost that year. 'The market for shares is thin and I wish I were on a few Boards where the Directors fees were as high,' Bradman wrote. 'Despite that, if you want a small speculation, it may well pay off.' He also liked meat companies Tancred Bros Industries and Anderson Meat Industries. Tancred had long been a favourite, he told Rivett, with great reserves on very little capital. And they would do better. 'World demand for meat must go up,' he wrote. 'The price of steak in USA and Japan is fantastic . . .' He also gave Permewan Wright a push – 'almost a faultless record' – even though Sir John Allison, whom Bradman considered a genius, had recently retired as chairman.

There was little boasting from Bradman about his record as an investment analyst, but he could not resist the occasional breakout. In September 1966 he quoted two paragraphs from a letter he had written to Rivett two years earlier about his view of the market. The quotes from 1964 began with Bradman saying he was not sanguine about its prospects – that government tax increases and rising input costs were hurting companies which otherwise looked like doing well, and that 'Uncle Tom' (Playford) clamping down on margins, regional political instability in Asia and the somewhat bearish interest rate outlook did not inspire confidence. The final quote from his 1964 letter ended: 'Will the mood persist to keep Kelvinators at 26/-?'

'Looking back I am a bit proud of that,' Bradman wrote to Rivett from the vantage point of September 1966. 'Kelvinators are 18/– & if I could always predict as accurately 2 years ahead, I would be grateful.' He noted the market had fallen and that, barring an unpredicted slump, there should be some recovery in prospect despite the relentlessly rising cost base of Australian business.

News seemed to be an exception to this fairly gloomy prognosis. As 1966 drew to a close, Rivett gave Bradman a negative assessment of News' corporate health. But Bradman had his own inside source, which he fancied as extremely close to the money. This source '*knows* things are looking better this year', Bradman told Rivett. 'He claims the *Australian* made a profit (genuine) last week, for the first time, & that News' figures this year so far are running 40% ahead of last.' News was likely to finish the year with figures 20 per cent better than the previous year, the source said. Perhaps things were not as gloomy as News' balance sheet suggested, Bradman mused; and in any case, Lord Thomson was thought to be in the wings.

In November 1966 Bradman and Rivett chewed over the latest figures on the Herald & Weely Times and Ansett. Bradman agreed the Herald result was good but wondered when the company would reveal as much profit as it could show if it stopped its excessive asset write-offs – assets already way below their book value. The Ansett balance sheet he found disturbing. 'I shuddered when I read his liabilities,' Bradman told Rivett. Ansett had $75 million due in liabilities within the next twelve months: 'Despite massive bank assistance & public borrowing, that is some debt.'

April 1967 saw a rare case of Bradman upbraiding Rivett on an investment matter. 'You never told me about W.M. [Western Mining] being recommended to you at 2.50,' he wrote. 'Nice time to tell me now. Touched 12.50 today.' Bradman again lauded the virtue of retailers. All shares fluctuate in value according to prevailing conditions, he said, but he had always been partial to retailers because they could buy from anyone and sell at a profit: 'The poor old manufacturer is at the mercy of many things and takes far greater risks.' Conversely, the best retailers should always do well, subject to the quality of their management. He declared Myer the best of them. Its low yield should not be a concern since strong capital appreciation was more valuable than taxable dividends, in his view. David Jones, Coles, Woolworths or even Youngs, a Canberra retailer, were worth a look. Not so John Martins, an Adelaide retailer: the outlook in South Australia was gloomy, and was drifting further since Labor had won the recent state election.

'Thank goodness clients can't sue brokers for bad advice on investments,' Bradman told Rivett. Rivett may live to see the day when he would be glad he had sold his Norseman shares at the price he had. Bradman quoted US financier Pierpont Morgan's 'self-proclaimed formula for making millions on the market: 'selling too soon'. Recent prices were 'farcical' and he was not alone in thinking so, Bradman wrote. Even so, Rivett was welcome to venture into real estate but Bradman would not be in it personally, he said – the prospective capital gains were accompanied by too many headaches.

What he could not understand, he told his friend, was the relentless rise in News shares, then trading at $2.05. Rivett had told Bradman that Murdoch was to close the *Australian*, but Bradman replied that Murdoch's own broker had assured Bradman that the paper would live on.

Bradman steered Rivett away from some speculative investments in June 1967, notably in Westralian Oil shares and in Ansett debentures. 'You are getting amongst the speculative boys when you talk about this company which produces mineral sands at Yoganup in WA,' Bradman wrote of Westralian Oil. The market for one obscure product it claimed to be developing was nebulous in Bradman's view and there were other question marks. 'They refer to the increase in their ore reserves, but I cannot find anywhere a reference to what their ore reserves are or were, and so I cannot figure out what an increase might mean.' Bradman told Rivett to stay away from dubious debentures: 'You might be wise to stick to the good ones and not be greedy for an extra 1%.' Bradman said he would not risk his own money in Ansett debentures despite the yield.

In July 1967 Rivett told Bradman he believed that News shares were being 'fixed'. Why, and by whom, Bradman wanted to know: 'In any case does that matter if someone continues to "fix" them up to $3?' Bradman said he was puzzled by the price of News, but equally so by the persistently weak price of Heralds followed by a brief, sharp uptick. Bradman told Rivett the grapevine said to hold the mining company Souths but that, after extensive personal inquiries by him recently in Sydney, engineering firm Evans Deakin did not seem to have much upside.

Around this time Bradman took Rivett back to the fundamentals he himself used to make investment decisions. There was no point buying shares yielding 4–5 per cent unless there was a better dividend, bonus, new issue or some other plus in prospect – otherwise one was better off with fixed interest investments yielding seven per cent. Dividend yield was not that important anyway, he argued, because of taxation. Far more important was the prospective yield and especially the earnings yield 'because a company cannot indefinitely earn say 30% & pay 10%'. Eventually, he said, something had to go to shareholders in that situation.

Against that backdrop Bradman compared Angus & Robertson with Rigby. He thought Angus & Robertson a good company but Rigby the better buy: its dividend cover and earnings yield were both superior and it was a more likely takeover prospect. 'There is a lot of luck in the takeover stakes but that is often where the big money lies,' he told Rivett. Similarly he preferred Faulding over Drug Houses of Australia as a buy.

He drew another lesson for Rivett in relation to Anderson Meat. 'Somehow when shares have a disastrous fall, recovery is often slower than anticipated,' Bradman wrote. The problem frequently lay in the quality of management and this was not easily solved. He recommended Rivett steer off Anderson Meat for that reason and buy Albert G Sims, which had also suffered a fall, instead. In the latter's case the fall was clear cut, the solution already in place and the outlook for earnings and yield now looked good.

Norseman was worth a dollar, but beyond that was 'pure gambling', he told Rivett. 'There will be some burnt fingers over nickel,' Bradman said presciently.

In August 1967 Bradman asked Rivett for the second time about the bright future forecast for the *Australian* by media executive and analyst Douglas Brass, of whom Rivett thought highly. Rivett had not responded to the initial query. 'In the meantime, of course, the paper is closed down because of the strike and now I am just wondering whether this may not even provide a heaven sent excuse for not opening it at all,' he wrote. Bradman had heard that Rivett thought Syme was good buying at current prices: was this correct? Bradman had seen the ABC television program 'Impact', featuring former editor of the *Australian* Maxwell Newton on Rupert Murdoch, and told Rivett he understood why

Rivett had enjoyed it so much. He agreed, too, that 'Newton did himself no good and that the ABC were rather kind to Murdoch'. You were wise, he told Rivett, not to have taken part.

Bradman's investment calls continued to be based on detailed information about what was happening on the ground in each of the sectors he followed. In August 1967 he gave a comprehensive rundown of meat stocks. Steer off Walker's, he advised: export-oriented companies like it were bearing heavy capital costs then to get their meatworks to meet government requirements. In addition, stock was in short supply and prices were high. Tancred looked good in the long term. He even recounted how Metro Meat in the tiny South Australian town of Old Noarlunga had just laid off half its workforce because of stock shortages.

He disagreed with Rivett on Norths and Souths. Rivett should hold onto Souths, he argued at length: its Queensland phosphate discovery was a potential bonanza, and its income was in any case coming increasingly from copper and less from lead and zinc.

The next day Bradman wrote again at twice the length, traversing an extraordinary number of stocks. He again urged his friend to trim his portfolio of straggling, speculative holdings. 'If you have shares in such things as Norths and Souths etc they really do the gambling for you in their speculating activities,' he wrote. 'Take oil for instance; it is significant that the really big find when it came was by BHP – not a small wild-cat. This is not surprising because the big boys have the best information.'

Every so often Bradman would draw his friend's attention to the situation likely to confront his family should anything happen to

Rohan. 'Without being morbid, and not knowing your personal affairs,' he wrote, 'unless you have sufficient other assets in cash (or equivalent) an untoward disaster to yourself might give your executors a headache if it happened on a high market and shares had to be sold after a fall.' It was something Rivett might think about discussing with his accountant or tax advisor, Bradman suggested, unless he had already dealt with this contingency.

Bradman revisited the issue in September and in October renewed an earlier theme concerning Rivett's risk orientation. Bradman nixed a Rivett sally for H. Deering which Bradman said he had always found difficult to sell, only managing to do so at a significant discount. Its image may have improved, Bradman wrote, but he had an inherent bias against investments lacking a ready market: 'I believe marketability has a value . . .' He went on to argue that 'high interest rates are illusory'. It was the net after tax that mattered.

A hypothetical purchase by Nan of 1000 Deering eight per cent notes ('poor security – poor marketability') was used by Bradman to make his point. Her marginal extra income would be $80 per annum, from which tax would have to be deducted. Say she bought 1000 Myer seven per cent notes ('good security – fully marketable') instead. Her marginal extra income would be $70 on which tax would also have to be paid. A lot of security and marketability would be sacrificed for barely any extra return, he argued.

A visit to Perth in October 1967 saw Bradman renewing his warning about fingers being burnt in the incipient nickel boom – to which he added oil. But from those he met and talked to in Western Australia, including Premier Charles Court, Bradman was 'sold' on the north-west. He nevertheless told Rivett that despite its fantastic price he would not hold Hamersley shares on the basis of what he had learned.

Canvassing other shares raised by Rivett at the time, he cautioned his friend against acquiring more shares in Rigby since 'short term moves may hold them back'. Since Bradman was a director of the company, this was perhaps sailing close to the wind. He was in any case very down on South Australia, where Rigby was headquartered at the time. He told Rivett things were 'b/awful' in South Australia, and that the contrast between there and Western Australia was extraordinary.

The following year Bradman told Rivett that if he were a young man he would be 'off like a shot' to Melbourne or Perth because of South Australia's declining prospects. His affection for his adopted home was nevertheless clear: 'I feel very sad that, irrespective of which Government is in power, I can see SA slipping back as against other states because of her lack of resources & advantages'.

In his correspondence Bradman was evocative not just in his imaginings of the future but also in his memories of the past. The reverberations of long ago events emerged in a letter to Rivett in August 1968 in which he continued his investment dialogue with Rivett. Things had been hectic, he said, but he had spoken with Bob Pentelow about Rivett's desired trades. Bradman explained to Rivett what he looked for in a stock, and why. The backdrop to his thinking concerned events from nearly forty years earlier: 'I still have vivid recollections of the interest reduction act 1930/2 . . .' This memory led Bradman to prefer shares with low nominal yields, preferably around five per cent, that were significantly below par and had a big asset backing. He went on to explain, however, that in several respects he preferred note and debenture opportunities even more. He used the example of a recent sale of Healing 7.25 per cent 1970 notes at $90, with an effective yield of 12 per cent and a tax-free capital increment; its fixed repayment date was also an advantage, he argued.

'The market gave some people a shock recently but those holding high priced speculative mining deserved it,' he wrote in October 1968. There were several industrials that also looked too high. How much longer, he wanted to know, could Australia absorb the Arbitration Court's rulings on wages, which in the then full employment environment continued apace?

By the late 1960s, Bradman's scepticism about the state of Australia's economy peaked. He believed much of the current share-buying was driven by inflationary fears. Rivett's 'clever Jew friend' – unnamed – had already been affected by an adverse move in Hamersley's share price, though Bradman thought the other major metals companies would be fine. Money was certain to lose purchasing power, he told Rivett, the only question was how quickly. What was more, the currency's decline would accelerate if the 'clowns' running the Arbitration Commission kept up their 'hand outs'.

'Our markets are sick,' he declared in the run-up to John Gorton's re-election as prime minister, which he forecast could generate a modest improvement – likewise, an easing of interest rates abroad. Nor were the trading gods favouring Bradman at that moment: there were good August rains, but they came after the family's sheep had already been sold at depressed prices.

But Bradman still liked News. 'I must be ignorant or bold – as you say – because I still hold a parcel of News,' he wrote in

November 1968. He did acknowledge Rivett's negative assessment of News' fundamentals, and added a caveat of his own: 'I don't like Rupert's move to England (if approved) but of course my answer is to sell – and stupidly perhaps I hang on.' But he fancied News as a potential takeover target, seeing a Packer or a Lord Thomson perhaps springing from the background and driving the share price up. Heralds and Queensland Press looked good, he exclaimed.

Rivett's good stock picks were acknowledged by his friend. In August 1969 Bradman told Rivett he had been right in his assessment of Mount Isa Mines and CSR, and that his comments about several other stocks had been 'on the ball'. As for the rest of the stocks canvassed in their recent correspondence, they were long term holding propositions – 'simply stocks to put away and forget'.

October 1969 saw another comprehensive pass at media stocks by Bradman who concluded Queensland Press was his 'No. 1' pick at that time. Rupert Murdoch might burnish his position with the acquisition of *News of the World* and the *Sun* in Britain, and 'his earning rate is pretty attractive', but he agreed with Rivett that News at $4.50 was somewhat overvalued. He did not agree with his media friend that it was a good time to buy David Syme, however, which Bradman predicted was set to lose money on an evening newspaper – one which he thought the Herald & Weekly Times would be prepared to spend extravagantly to counter in defence of its Melbourne *Herald*.

The markets would make for interesting watching in the new year, Bradman told Rivett. He forecast a credit squeeze and even higher interest rates: 'And how the mining speculators can go on at this rate is beyond me.' BHP was the stock to stick with, he said.

Bradman returned to the theme a fortnight later: 'For some

time I have been thinking that there is madness in the share market.' Some of the miners could actually prove undervalued even at current prices. He cited MIM as an example. Some of the newer stocks may amount to something eventually but most, he argued, would never pay a dividend and investors would lose their money on them. The challenge was to be able to pick the likely duds. If he were in that sort of market, Bradman told Rivett, 'my main concern would be to see that no matter what happened I couldn't lose'.

He advised Rivett to hold his Onkaparinga shares in case the firm issued a bonus for its impending one hundredth anniversary. Bradman was downbeat, however, about Bradford Insulation which faced competition from synthetic insulation, especially in refrigeration. Foam was fast displacing slag wool, he wrote, revealing his usual eye for operating detail.

Another fortnight hence, despite something of a correction, the market still seemed demented to Bradman. 'Surely though it can't be long before some common sense enters the arena,' he wrote. 'Shares float at 10c & quickly go to $1 without any justification. It is sheer madness.'

Adelaide Steamship's share price was up on a rumoured takeover offer, but Bradman reminded Rivett of H.C. Sleigh's ill-fated attempt to acquire the firm several years earlier. It was rejected and the company never really recovered from the three for one share bonus that followed.

South Australia's attractions as an investment destination declined sharply under Don Dunstan's premiership, in Bradman's view. In June 1970 he told Rivett he would not buy any Adelaide-based stocks, not even Advertiser Newspapers. The *Advertiser* had 'gone to hell' as a paper and was troubled by unprofitable subsidiaries. Heralds or Queensland Press were preferable. Argo, a highly diversified firm, was an exception. Irresponsible union behaviour, especially in the manufacturing sector, made him cautious about industrials in general: 'It is hell today trying to cope with all the problems in business.'

The amount of investment commentary focused on individual stocks diminished sharply in the letters surviving from the early 1970s. Personal matters dominated. But even as Bradman grappled with the very public trauma of John changing his surname by deed poll to 'Bradsen', and was too down to discuss much else, he managed a caution on Adelaide Motors shares – fully priced, at '70'c, he and Bob Pentelow agreed after a long discussion the previous week.

In late 1973 Bradman gave Rivett a general appreciation of the investment outlook – realistically gloomy given emerging economic trends and the by now established governance mode of the Whitlam administration. Having reviewed Rivett's share portfolio, he judged it so diversified as to eliminate any foreseeable weakness.

But the situation called for a rethinking of the then perception of shares as a hedge against inflation – that asset values and profits would increase in line with inflation. Profits were now at 'considerable risk' because of government regulation, and even government attempts to influence asset values. Asset values were, in any case, often only theoretically relevant, Bradman argued, citing Myer's Bourke Street, Melbourne, store value as a case in point. Whatever its value, Myer needed the store from which to conduct its business, so the fact that it might be worth four times its book value was not centrally relevant. 'So I feel we have to think hard about the modern concept of just what is a true hedge against inflation,' Bradman wrote.

After a big rise in interest rates and fall in share prices, the stockmarket rallied slightly at the end of October. Bradman's theory was that the rise was on rumours that Whitlam may call an early election – rumours which Bradman himself dismissed. Instead he forecast more federal government regulation that would 'wreck the business community far more than they have done already'. Get rid of Ampol shares, he argued, given its debt, and the possibility of petrol price controls and loss of exploration tax breaks. 'Not sure about Symes but you would be better informed,' he closed.

Bradman was an active director well into his older years. On the verge of sixty-seven years old, he ran the Argo group while its chairman Alf Adamson was on an extended trip abroad. At the same time he accepted the trusteeship of a major superannuation fund which had 'special problems'.

Inflation and its collateral damage for employers, employees and investors not only made the life of company directors like Bradman several degrees harder, it also decreased the attractiveness of the stockmarket. Bradman declared in November 1976, 'property is the best in an inflationary era'. The corollary was obvious. 'As to the question of ordinary shares being an attractive investment for the private individual, the evidence points to a considerable reduction both in merit and in enthusiasm,' he told Rivett. 'More and more shares are flowing into the hands of institutions, superannuation funds and the like.' In BHP's case, he wrote, the number of names on the share register had fallen by 14 per cent in just over a year: 'Moreover, the costs of buying and selling a small parcel are now so high that one needs a market improvement of 10% to get square. These factors have virtually eliminated the speculator from the market.'

Bradman saw continuing downward pressure on Australia's exchange rate because of the high cost structures built into the economy during the Whitlam period. 'We have now come from some 35% below USA costs to 35% above, practically anything can be imported more cheaply from overseas than it can be manufactured locally,' he said. Moreover Whitlam's 'virtual abolition' of tax concessions for mining and oil development investment had wiped out a key source of funds, and capital costs in the sector were now prohibitive.

The Fraser Government was correct in making the fight against inflation its priority, Bradman told Rivett, 'because if that is not won nothing else will matter'. But he saw strong pressure on the government from its Country Party coalition partner for devaluation, which would undercut the anti-inflation effort; he noted that capital continued to surge out of Australia despite Fraser's efforts.

Ever mindful of new legislative obligations on advisors and directors, Bradman ended the letter in which he reviewed more than two dozen companies for Rivett with a long disclaimer. '[I] want to emphasize that in the light of the current legislation as to giving advice, this is sent E&OE and without prejudice and in the knowledge that I am not any longer in the business, am not an expert, and am only replying to a query from a friend,' he wrote. 'If you listen to any of my advice, you do so at your own peril. But at least I might have given you something to think about.'

A few weeks before he died, Rivett acknowledged just how

good Bradman's analysis and judgement had been in relation to his portfolio. 'Before I finish let me say again how accurate your estimates of shares I am interested in has proved,' Rivett wrote, unaware it would be his final appreciation of Bradman's advice. Bradman may have been a little tough on one stock in the thirty-odd he had assessed for his friend 'but on all other points you and the market have been in agreement'.

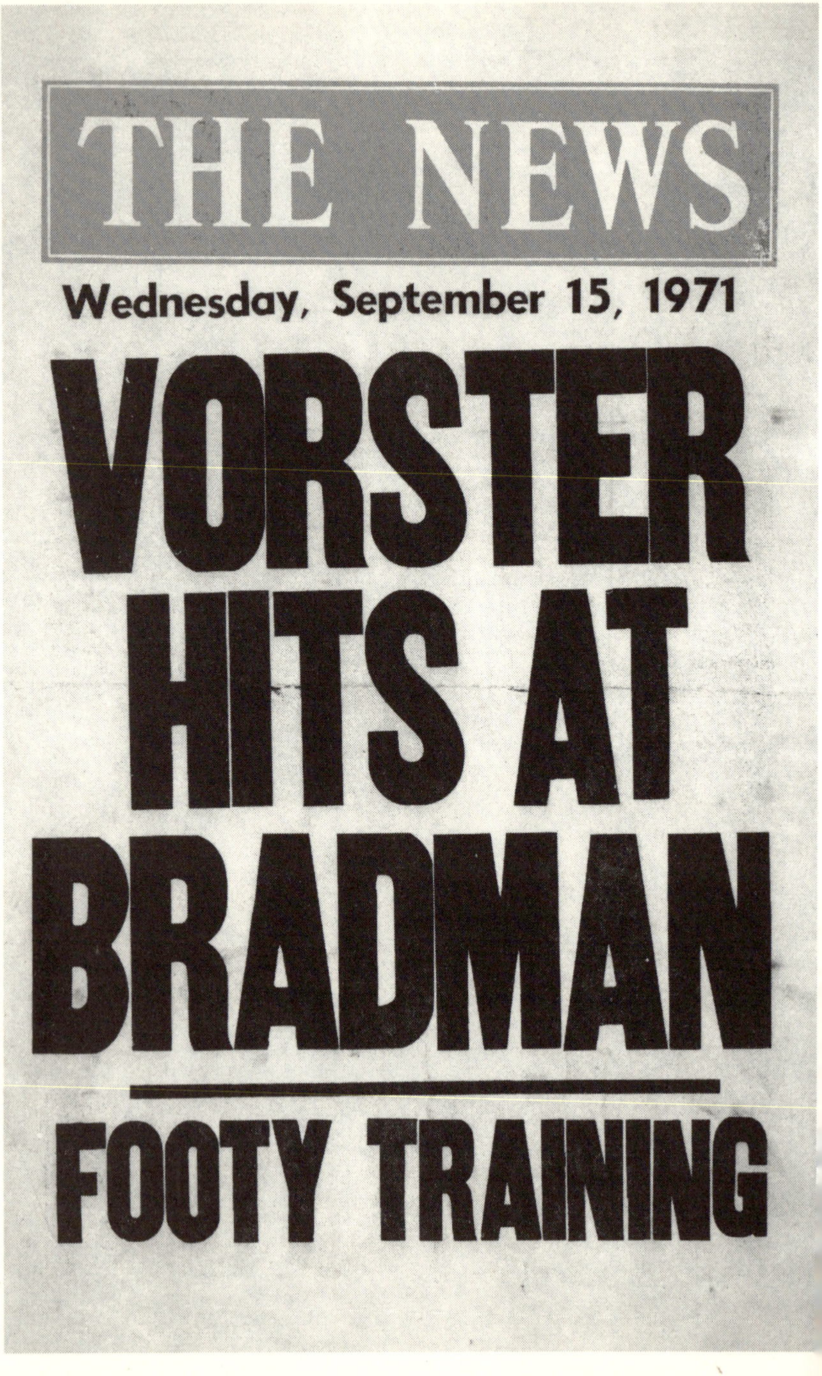

THE NEWS

Wednesday, September 15, 1971

VORSTER HITS AT BRADMAN

FOOTY TRAINING

4 *Politics*

'. . . my political philosophy does not support any party but only the personal things which I believe in.'

— Don Bradman

Bradman lived in South Australia through the long era of Liberal Country League (LCL) rule by Sir Thomas Playford and his successor, Steele Hall, followed by the national pace-setting Labor government of Don Dunstan. The letters make it clear that Bradman was non-party political. He was sceptical about politicians in general and Playford, whom he called 'Uncle Tom' in his letters to Rivett, was no exception. Long-serving Australian prime minister Sir Robert Menzies he regularly referred to by his unflattering war-time sobriquet of 'Ming'.

Adelaide's small-townness, and the incestuous binding up of the media with the wielding of power, was well understood by Bradman. 'Why – The News is attacking Playford again,' he wrote Rivett in July 1962. 'The Editor had better be careful or he'll find himself in Brazil or somewhere.' It was another allusion to Rupert Murdoch's arbitrary use of proprietorial power which he knew would provide succour to the wounded Rivett.

Rivett's seemingly swashbuckling existence as a journalist on the international stage in Zurich, travelling widely and eagerly engaged in world affairs, appealed mightily to Bradman. 'You must be having such an interesting life . . . but exasperating when turmoil persists all around us,' he wrote in June 1962. 'There seems no prospect of real peace in our lifetime.'

That Bradman kept in touch with world political developments as much as domestic Australian ones is evident in his regular references to them in the letters. He was acutely aware of the interaction between politics, the economy and share prices. Politics was one key motivation for Bradman's regular cautions against buying shares in the airline Ansett, which operated in one of the most regulated sectors in the economy and was therefore vulnerable to changes in government policy. 'The political background makes me have a bias against Ansetts and of course a Labor Gov't would try and wreck him,' he told Rivett in July 1963. He was also sensitive to international developments. In the same letter he said that he would hate Rivett to sell his shares in Timor Oil just before they had a find but said he had a feeling that Indonesia's President Soekarno 'may get there first'. Or US President Kennedy might make a mess of some stocks if he decided to 'unload much of his 8 billion dollars surplus stockpile' of US currency on the market.

But notions that Bradman was by conviction a Liberal or Country Party supporter are refuted by the letters. He is sceptical about conservative and Labor politicians alike, and regularly critical of government and opposition policy approaches. Again in the same letter Bradman mused that if Prime Minister Robert Menzies won the next election and things settled down, he would not be surprised if repressive economic measures were applied quite quickly: 'In my book the taps will be turned on for perhaps 6 to 12 months but if inflation looks like taking over again, the banks will put the screws on.' And Australian business was already finding it harder to be profitable than the relative buoyancy of the market suggested, he added.

This theme continued as the 1960s wore on. Somehow, wrote Bradman, 'my suspicious nature still doesn't make me believe that either political party is "well meaning".' Bradman's politics were analysed essentially through an investor prism, and he was critical of policies adversely affecting the investor outlook – and these criticisms came under both Liberal and Labor administrations, without discriminating between the two. During the devastating stagflation of the mid-1970s he extended this into a fervent concern that workers' jobs be saved.

For Bradman the struggle he believed business had making profits was the underlying issue. Some of his insights foretold the Hawke Government's economic agenda in the 1980s. One example was Bradman's belief that the Australian economy was not isolated from the world economy, and therefore could not be insulated for long from the flow-on effects of international economic developments. Another was his concern that wage increases occurred without reference to productivity improvements – something that the Hawke Government moved on in its enterprise bargaining push in the late 1980s.

He was trenchantly critical of the economic management of both the Menzies Government nationally and the Playford Government at the state level – both conservative administrations. 'I am not at all sanguine about future prosperity,' he told Rivett in September 1964. 'Every time the companies look like doing really well, the Government ups the tax, the basic wage goes up, charges such as 'phones are increased, and really you have got to push up sales every year to break even on profits. On top of that in South Australia, Uncle Tom clamps down on margins. If we really have a bit of shooting up Malaya way, if Harold Wilson gets in or if [Menzies Government Treasurer] Holt brings down an interim budget, there is plenty of room for this market to fall.'

Bradman sensed the changing of the guard, both on the world stage and at home. 'As for politics, I see Nehru is gone,' he wrote to Rivett. 'With Kennedy no more, Macmillan finished & Menzies ageing, we are confronted by new men. Where are we heading?' While the outlook was uncertain, there was nothing he or Rivett could do about it, he observed. Except perhaps attend testimonial dinners. 'Going to a dinner for Uncle Tom tonight,' he wrote Rivett in March 1965. 'Sir Lloyd [Dumas] organised it as a tribute from his loyal supporters.'

Bradman was deeply concerned by developments in British public policy in the mid-1960s. The 1965 UK budget made Bradman thank his lucky stars that he lived in Australia, though he feared similar government imposts could be imposed here eventually. Bradman asked Rivett to send his copy of *The Times* so that he could check the detail of the British budget, especially how the new capital gains tax would work.

Other international developments were keenly followed in light of their possible impact on cricket. 'Your views on Rhodesia frightened me but I somehow have faith that S. Africa won't be plunged into war to interrupt the cricket tour,' he wrote Rivett in October 1965. He admitted he had no logical basis for the belief other than that war had been in prospect in various places during that time, and the hostile parties had seemed to pull back from the brink of a 'holocaust'. The Bay of Pigs stand-off between the US and the Soviet Union had occurred only two years earlier.

Bradman kept up with politics beyond the strict news sense. He read the excerpts of a lecture given by Menzies in October 1965, reproduced in one of the daily newspapers, and told Rivett he thought they read quite well: 'Did Ming entertain you?' On world affairs he continued to defer to Rivett's greater depth of knowledge and experience: 'The world is about to be plunged into another crisis over Rhodesia, a situation which you understand far better than I do . . .'

One certainty, Bradman felt from the vantage point of 1966, was a capital gains tax at some point in the future. Price controls were also a possibility, and would be difficult to shake off if introduced, he told Rivett. 'But I am becoming more philosophical & inclined to say let's be thankful for today than ever I was,' he wrote. 'Who can see the future?' The Whitlam Government was subsequently unsuccessful in a 1974 referendum to gain constitutional power for wage and price controls. The Hawke Government did, however, establish a capital gains tax, as Bradman foresaw, nearly twenty years later in 1985.

Bradman was highly critical of government economic management – and this was during an extended period of Liberal Party rule at both the federal and state levels. His personal philosophy was certainly a fairly conservative one of self-reliance, and he opposed Australians' proneness to cut down tall poppies. 'The modern tendency to sympathise with those who suffer misfortune and frown on those who are successful is, to me, putting the cart before the horse,' he wrote. But he thought the Liberal administrations then dominating Australian politics were singularly ineffective in delivering the right policies and climate for a prosperous nation. 'We need successful and prosperous businesses but almost everything the Governments do seems to make it harder for business. Certainly at present in the spheres in which I move, making a profit is a really difficult matter. The mounting costs in a variety of ways can only be countered by rising sales and when they fall (as they are doing) it is difficult.' Retail sales in Sydney were down nine per cent in the most recent quarter, he told Rivett; the appliance field was 'chaotic', and competition generally was fierce.

Like capital gains, Bradman also correctly foresaw the significant reliance governments would develop on energy taxes. Much as he would oppose it, Bradman told Rivett, 'I feel one of the certain tax increases before long will be on petrol.' There was so little left to tax which could generate major revenue, he said, and Australia's petrol was at that time cheap compared to other countries.

There was a persistent sense in Bradman of powerlessness against disturbing world developments. In September 1966 Bradman thanked Rivett for his comments on Indonesia in a recent letter. The world was poised for further instability, Bradman said, reiterating his view that peace, in the sense that they had previously understood it, was not in prospect. 'Providing we can contain events into local scrub fires all will be well,' he wrote. 'But a sudden change of wind and any fire may get out of hand. It used to worry me but what can I do?' He would leave it to the politicians, whatever happened.

In late 1966 Rivett visited Manila and Bradman sought his views on development there. 'Meanwhile I guess we are all relieved that [US President] LBJ left Australia in one piece, alive,'

Bradman wrote about Lyndon Baines Johnson's visit. Then there was the forthcoming federal election: 'Not a very exciting choice but nevertheless one cannot but fear an Australia led by [Arthur Calwell] . . .' A Calwell government would be too prone to union influence, he argued, worsening the business input costs creep he had worried about for years. The problem was already entrenched under state and federal Liberal administrations: Bradman predicted that Australian companies' bottom lines would in any case deteriorate during 1967 but he felt the situation would be even worse under Calwell.

He need not have worried. November brought not only an unexpected Shield match victory by South Australia over Western Australia, but an unexpectedly big win by Liberal Prime Minister Harold Holt over Calwell. Bradman segued seamlessly between the two events in one paragraph. 'Not satisfied with his belting, [Calwell] does his block & lambasts Pres. Johnson for congratulating Holt & saying America will stand by Australia,' he wrote to Rivett. 'I think Arthur must have gone off the beam.'

The federal Labor opposition was a shambles, in Bradman's view, and this was a problem especially in light of the Liberals' arrogance even before Holt's overwhelming victory: 'This is of course bad because Australia can do with a good stable middle of the road party and it won't help to have a party in power with such a big majority.' Rivett had told Bradman he distrusted the Gallup Poll as run by Roy Morgan Research in Australia, but Bradman said he thought its call on the 1966 election had turned out to be very accurate. 'I was distrustful once too,' he wrote, 'but in recent years I've felt they get pretty close to the pulse of things.'

Rivett enjoyed provoking Bradman politically, and the letters show Bradman enjoying the provocation. One person designated a Bradman mate was not, Bradman declared, but 'I am a friend of [cricketer Bill] Lawry & . . . I don't get mixed up in politics, left or right,' he weighed in after an especially good Rivett stir. Nor did the fact that John Kenneth Galbraith had written something in the *Observer* make it necessarily correct – any more correct than 'university opinion' that pegged Galbraith as a second class, one-eyed economist. Bradman repeated the long running gag line between the two men, first used by Rivett against Bradman: Why didn't he give up reading the 'bloody Bully' (the *Bulletin* magazine)? Bradman's practical thinking had proved superior to Rivett's theory, netting him $2 as a result of a bet between them. What, Bradman wanted to know, could they bet on next?

The likelihood of a hike in energy taxes was raised again by Bradman in June 1967 when commenting on road hauler Yellow Express as a possible investment raised by Rivett. 'It wouldn't [surprise] me either if we had a fairly stiff lift in the price of petrol. When you come to think of the price of petrol here compared with England or the Continent it must be a big bait for the Commonwealth Government.'

Bradman believed that Labor governments were inclined to want to constrain the media. In August 1967 he responded to Rivett's comment about the troubled atmosphere of Sydney journalism, where strike action had broken out. No matter, said Bradman – the journalists would go back to work when their money ran out. 'I would regard a bigger threat is Whitlam's promise to start up newspapers when he gets in plus Dunstan's announcement that he has asked the Prices Commissioner to investigate prices etc of the Adelaide press,' he wrote. 'That's what they get for giving him such favourable publicity.' Labor's desire and intention to trim the media's sails was crystal clear, according to Bradman, who believed the party would 'move heaven and earth to clip the wings of today's press people'.

Dunstan and his cohorts had done a magnificent job getting the media interstate to attack Playford's successor as Liberal state premier, Steele Hall, Bradman told Rivett. He noted that Rivett did not seem to like Hall, Hall's party or the gerrymander that kept the Liberals in power in South Australia. No-one likes a gerrymander, he went on, unless it favoured the party they supported: the 'Labor boys didn't squeal in Q. or NSW whilst *their* gerrymander kept them in power'.

What about Whitlam, he asked his friend. 'Gorton doesn't impress me but seems to impress others,' Bradman continued. As the 1960s drew to a close he was consistent in his even-handed scepticism about both sides of politics. His approach to public policy was always through the lens of what was best for investment, and therefore what was best for business, but this did not spill over into partisan support for the Liberal Party. 'I guess politics are important but they sicken me because of their insincerity,' he told Rivett. 'I prefer to interest myself, or should I say *involve* myself, in other matters . . .'

The politics of race in South Africa loomed as a major issue for those involved in international cricket. It was one Bradman could not avoid being drawn into, but he brought a cricket-centric view to his thinking on it. In October 1968 he told Rivett that, like Rivett, he felt 'a bit sick' about recent events in South Africa as cricket there began to be drawn into the anti-apartheid struggle, but went on to say this was simply because of its effect on the game. Bradman said he did not understand the situation properly, or who was to blame, but that he was to meet with the South African Board's president that day to discuss the situation.

Around this time Bradman tried to draw out Rivett on his current views on Australian politics. The real problem, Bradman wrote, was that he did not know anymore whom Rivett supported in the domestic political scene. Bradman's own views remained trenchant, in relation to the inadequate conduct of economic policy at least. Exchange rates worldwide were in a mess, he wrote in November 1968, and all because of 'government mismanagement'. He was no more impressed with the way things were being run at home, under Liberal Prime Minister John Gorton: 'Inflation is inevitable at an increasing rate & the idiots running our arbitration system are leading us to ruin.' These things 'drive me nuts', he wrote.

John Gorton's narrow federal election win in October 1969 saw Bradman sledge the federal coalition parties and its leaders as, essentially, slackers. He referred on this occasion to the federal Liberals and their coalition partners, then called the Country Party and later renamed the Nationals, as the 'LCL' – the Liberal and Country League, the name under which the fusion of the two conservative parties in South Australia then operated. This was incorrect, but in the context there is no doubting to whom Bradman referred.

'It will give a few of the LCL boys a headache & make them get off their tails, though I wonder if anything could make Gorton get off his tail,' Bradman wrote after the result came in. 'I have a feeling now that LCL must get a new young leader fast (who I wouldn't know) or they are headed for the wilderness next time. I just can't see Gorton winning another election.'

Bradman was right about Gorton. He did not win another

federal election, losing the leadership before the 1972 election to the somewhat absurd figure of William McMahon, who narrowly lost to Labor's Gough Whitlam. Contrary to modern perceptions of a landslide win, Whitlam's majority was modest.

Consistent with his general sentiment that neither side of politics was up to the task, Bradman also criticised the likely consequences of Labor wins state and federally. South Australian Opposition Leader Don Dunstan was certain to win the next state election, he told Rivett, predicting big increases in gift duty, estate duties and the like from Labor in office. A federal Labor win would similarly lead to a capital gains tax, surtax and complementary measures 'quick smart'.

Was there no way to get efficient government, Bradman despaired, with less waste and fewer public servants? He anticipated the rhetoric of the federal coalition Fraser Government in the 1970s, and the swinging cost-cutting of the federal Labor Hawke Government in the 1980s, constraining public sector growth.

Bradman regularly underlined his hostility to politicians in general, not just to those from any particular party. 'I hate politicians as a race but beyond all else I hate those who sit on the fence & try to use things for political advantage contrary to their convictions,' he wrote in June 1970. The comment was triggered by British Labour Prime Minister Harold Wilson's election loss. Bradman was laid up sick in bed: 'But I'm not too sick to gloat over Wilson's defeat.' Bradman believed Wilson's involvement in cricket politics was instrumental in the collapse of a Test series between England and South Africa, and was a vote loser for him. Yet Bradman perceived correctly that South African cricket had been irrevocably politicised, and that he would have to face the same issue as Wilson. 'The thing now is "What do we do about Africa here in 1971/2?" This is a really serious question,' he went on. 'If you were in my shoes what action would you be taking?'

As Bradman aged and his program remained demanding, and even intensified, exhaustion became a constant companion. In September 1971 he told Rivett his 'depression' about the future made him bleaker than ever about politics, even though he found Rohan's comments concerning Canberra interesting in his recent letter. He despaired that there was nothing on offer but 'unpalatable alternatives' in the political sphere. Liberal Prime Minister William McMahon and Labor Opposition Leader Gough Whitlam were the choices on offer. Bradman was tired of distorted reporting – it made him 'give up the ghost' on matters of public life. Or was it just old age, he queried.

However it might weary him though, an intense interest in public policy and its better conduct continued. Four months after the Whitlam Government's election he railed that business was getting more difficult every day and that conditions were set to worsen rapidly. But he did not link it to Labor's election. Rather he saw the to him obvious economic problems emerging as part of a longer term pattern of inadequate policy and economic management in Australia. 'It looks like an inflationary explosion looming up,' he predicted correctly in March 1973. 'I've been forecasting this as enemy No.1 for ages and see no evidence that the responsible people have the remotest idea of controlling it.'

As the Whitlam Government continued in office, however, critical jabs began to crop up regularly in the correspondence. 'Whitlam permitting' he would see Rivett soon in Melbourne,

Bradman wrote in July 1973 in a likely reference to soaring industrial disputation at the time. A few months later Bradman made a crack about Whitlam Government Treasurer Frank Crean, writing about something he would do 'unless I am bankrupted before then by Crean & Co'. By October 1973 the criticism intensified: 'All I know is that if [Gough] stays there much longer we'll all be broke . . .' Bradman put the modest stockmarket rally in late October down to early election rumours, not that he thought one likely: 'I doubt if Labor will risk one and the odds are they will stay in power and wreck the business community far more than they have done already.'

But as the Whitlam Government's depths as economic managers were plumbed, Bradman condemned the government's incompetence but still rejected attempts to box him into any party political corner. Rivett wrote in May 1975 that their political views had hardly been harmonious. 'I don't know whether that is true or not,' Bradman replied. 'I don't know exactly what your views are . . . and you couldn't know mine because my political philosophy does not support any party but only the personal things which I believe in.'

Bradman was stunned at the economic damage being wrought at that time, and told Rivett that it had massively increased the demands on him as a company director. 'I wouldn't mind if my time was taken up doing helpful and constructive things but so much of it is consumed trying to cope with the most absurd and useless regulations imposed on us by the present Government,' he wrote. 'It is almost unbelievable that so-called intelligent human beings could be responsible for some of our current legislation.'

The Trade Practices Act passed by parliament the previous year was a case in point, Bradman argued. A company in which he was then a director had sought advice on a trade practices matter concerning an agreement with another company. Independently, both companies obtained legal advice on whether the agreement complied with the Trade Practices Act. The two sets of advice directly contradicted each other, with one legal firm advising it complied and the other saying it breached the Act. The company of which Bradman was a director then asked the Deputy Commissioner's office of the Trade Practices Commission and was told they didn't know – it was up to the courts to decide. 'That's dandy,' Bradman fumed to Rivett. 'The penalty is up to $250,000 for the Company and $50,000 for the individual and nobody can tell you what the bloody Act means.'

In his earlier letter Rivett argued that Australia's international standing had been enhanced by the Whitlam Government. Bradman was dismissive of this in the context of what he saw as its attempt to 'wreck the private enterprise system' in Australia. Bradman confessed that he might be cynical but the admiration of international political leaders for Whitlam counted little 'when I am desperately striving to see that companies don't have to sack too many employees, or go bankrupt because of his ruinous domestic policies'.

Bradman was 'absolutely appalled' at Australia's economic outlook under Whitlam, he told Rivett. The government was culpable for letting inflation – almost all home grown, not imported, he argued – get out of control and for allowing the trade unions to dominate business. Bradman railed at the 'decades of hard work destroyed, apparently ruthlessly and deliberately' during Whitlam's watch. 'Regrettably,' he wrote, 'I see no cause for optimism under *any* Government (without union backing for a halt to wage increases – which seems a hopeless prospect).'

The empirical evidence supporting Bradman's criticisms speaks for itself. Former Treasury economist Dr Don Russell, a long time senior advisor to Labor Treasurer and Prime Minister Paul Keating, clearly sketched the scale of the problem. 'The economic statistics for 1974-5 tell the story: public sector outlays grew by 37 percent as a result of the 1974 [Jim] Cairns Budget; average weekly earnings grew by 25 percent, while the Consumer Price Index rose by 17 percent,' recalls Russell, who experienced the economic chaos from his perspective as a junior Treasury official. 'The dislocation to the Budget and the economy was immense.'

Bradman's prescription – low inflationary growth underpinned by 'union backing for a halt to wage increases' turned out not to be the 'hopeless prospect' he considered it in June 1975. The Hawke Labor Government was elected on just such a platform eight years later, in 1983. It embarked on a major modernisation of economic policy in Australia, with union-backed wage restraint in the 'Accord' its foundation.

'I think in my life I've steered a pretty middle course in politics, in business, and in life; I've tasted Kipling's two imposters, but my friends are far more numerous among the rank and file than the upper crust,' Bradman wrote. 'All in all I wouldn't have it any other way. And whether you agree with me politically or not I'll still be delighted to crack a bottle or two with our friends the Rivetts, either here or there, at the first opportunity. Hope it won't be too long.'

Bradman consciously perceived himself as middle of the road. Rivett, he briefly quipped in the letter, was more what would later become known as a 'chardonnay socialist' – rich enough to be able to afford left-wing political positions in public while having the preoccupations and pleasures of the rich in private. The letter led to a measured but comprehensive rebuke from Rivett, and a slight chilling of relations on Rivett's side.

The cooler relations did not last long. Six months later the correspondents engaged in friendly debate about the newly elected Fraser Government. As he had told Rivett on many previous occasions, 'I have no politics . . .' yet had no choice but to take some interest and, ultimately, a position in the national interest.

'That is why I found it necessary to work for the defeat of Whitlam (though I'm sorry for the way it was done) & why I supported Fraser,' Bradman wrote. 'I don't know Fraser, but to date I am disappointed by his performance . . .' This was perhaps because of ignorance about the enormity of the challenge facing Fraser behind the scenes as the new prime minister settled into his first few weeks of elected office, he said: 'All I know is that somebody, somehow, sometime *must* conquer inflation or the whole community, labor and libs, will be ruined.'

Bradman pointed out that he had been highlighting the dangers of inflation facing Australia since 1971 and was relieved that the public was beginning to realise its significance. It was not the first time he had mentioned it and Rivett, in a previous letter, had also identified the flailing McMahon Government as sewing the demon seed of inflation. Neither acknowledged, however, their agreement about the origins of the inflation so ferociously stoked by fiscal and wages policy under Whitlam.

Extortionate union demands and government deficits were to blame, Bradman argued, describing deficits as a confidence trick and wage claims in excess of productivity gains an automatic inflation booster: 'England today is a prime example of these twin evils which have wrecked that marvellous old land in the short space of 30 years.' But Bradman was no ideological union basher. 'I am in favour of unions if they are well run & sensible,' he added.

A realistic appreciation of how hard it would be to fix Australia's economic problems emerged later that year. Bradman told Rivett in October 1976 that his company directorships remained 'frustrating and worrying'. The economy suffered serious structural damage under Whitlam, he argued, and the necessary remedies were probably unacceptable to 'powerful groups and probably to the people as a whole'. Righting the economy would therefore be done the slow and painful way, he predicted.

'Society doesn't seem to work under a Hitler, a Stalin, a Wilson or a Ford,' Bradman commented, covering so much ground politically that it is hard to see, philosophically, what options remained. The correct path was to strive for what was 'right and proper' – a quest on which he told Rivett he had nearly given up. Cricket was the last realm in which he continued to try.

An article sent by Bradman to Rivett at that time, in October 1976, suggests that Bradman had not really stopped trying to persuade people to 'right and proper' positions at all. It concerned the ideas of libertarian Austrian economist Friedrich Hayek, the philosophical driving force behind the anti-inflation push common to English-speaking polities from the mid-1970s on.

Rivett returned it later that month, in case Bradman wanted to circulate the article to others. 'I have no doubt Keynes was very brilliant and one of the giants of the first third of this century,' Rivett wrote of Hayek's rival as the most influential economist of the twentieth century. 'But at times I feel his theories have led to as much harm as good.' This came in the context of a discussion between the two men about the erosion of the Australian currency's value due to inflation.

The doubts Rivett expressed about Keynesianism did not stop him proposing a classic Keynesian initiative in the same letter: the building of a six-lane highway between Melbourne and Sydney. 'This would be intelligent capital expenditure and has been advocated ever since the early 60s when that Texan US Ambassador – Allen – urged that a six lane highway between the two cities was a first priority essential,' Rivett wrote. 'How right he was and how stupid we look so many years later with tens of thousands of decent blokes out of a job and still no damned highway.'

Bradman's preoccupation with inflation and productivity would have made him apply those two tests to the Allen proposal. They were the two tests persistently applied to economic and allied policy decisions by the Hawke Labor government from 1983, beyond the time frame of the Bradman–Rivett correspondence. Bradman's economic policy predictions and Rivett's foreign policy leanings were, arguably, reconciled and implemented by the Hawke government. Not that this would have made Bradman a Labor man any more than he was a Liberal. He was neither – consciously and deliberately so. To him it was the ideas and the policies embodying them that were the important things.

5 *The Media*

'. . . the press, with its monopolistic control, has a bounded duty to preserve, uplift & encourage the features of humanity which are good.'
— Don Bradman

Bradman's engagement by Rivett to cover the 1953 Test series in England for the *News* is the subject of the very first letter in the series. He undertook to provide full coverage of the Tests, with News Limited holding world rights to the copy. The payment terms were outlined in Rivett's letter commissioning the coverage, which is not included in the series.

The very next letter, written on *Daily Mail* letterhead from Northcliffe House on 25 June 1953, was sent just before the Lord's Test. It contains significant insights into how Bradman thought cricket should be covered by the media, and shows him dealing in a very direct manner with Rivett the editor on journalistic matters.

There had been a logistical hitch getting Bradman's copy to the *News* in a timely fashion. Bradman expressed surprise and said the cabling arrangements – the source of the problem – had been a matter between the *News'* Rivett and the *Daily Mail*'s editor, not him. Bradman reported that, in any case, he had conferred with the

Daily Mail's Schofield that day and said the cables containing his Lord's copy would arrive by the *News*' deadline.

Despite Bradman's reluctance, Rivett had sold coverage to interstate morning newspapers to spread the *News*' costs, and Bradman had the same problem faced by any journalist covering a big international event with rights being sold on to other outlets. Since the *News* was an afternoon tabloid, this meant Bradman had to file at both ends of the day. Bradman told Rivett he was really most concerned with providing copy to the *News* and, in England, the *Daily Mail*, but that since Rivett had done the deal 'I shall do my best to help you out'. This meant some awkwardness, he explained. The following Saturday Australian Prime Minister Robert Menzies was holding a dinner for the team in London, and Rivett's deal meant that Bradman would have to file his story before the dinner, not write and send it in on the Sunday morning as he would have preferred.

The steps involved in filing the copy compounded the timing issues. Bradman explained he had to phone in his stories from the test grounds to a copytaker in the *Daily Mail*'s office in London. From there the copy would be cabled to Australia.

Rivett was clearly pleased with Bradman's copy, and the *News*' most gilt-edged of cricket correspondents welcomed the praise and thanked the editor for his comments. Some observations, however, Bradman batted back. Rivett had referred to 'Miller's indiscretion' which Bradman said was not an indiscretion at all but simply an accident. 'Rest assured I shall comment on such things if I think them worthy but I won't manufacture criticism,' he wrote. It was a conversation familiar to all journalists: the reporter on the spot trying to corral the distant editor prone to taking liberties with events as reported and attempting to impose their own interpretation on future copy.

Assuaging Rivett, Bradman followed this with the assurance that, on the other hand, he must surely report things like Simpson's catch – 'a virtual miracle'. Nor would he weigh his copy down with reportage of dull but worthy cricket; the final two hours' play on the last day of the Nottingham Test did not merit reporting, he said. Unless he was committing a significant error, Bradman asked Rivett to trust him as an observer on the ground 'to appreciate the vital moments'. He needed to be trusted, too, to provide full coverage over the course of the series. Bradman explained he had not rushed in and commented on strategy at 'Notts' because not everything could be written at once. Rather he wanted to wait for the Test strategy to emerge more fully during the series before commenting on and assessing it.

The greatest practical difficulty was posed by the 7.15 pm deadline to phone copy through to the *Daily Mail*. Play did not end until 6.30 pm. It was impossible to write a complete summary of the day's play in forty-five minutes, and Bradman had to make a solid start during the day. This problem would have been well known to Rivett but his cricket correspondent required no counsel, having come up with the obvious solution right away.

Bradman expressed pleasure that his copy wasn't being pirated by other media outlets: 'I don't know whether that would be because of the legal warning or whether they think Bradman's stuff is not worth pinching anyhow, but at least it saves you a bit of worry . . . It looks as though I have found the secret of avoiding newspapermen.'

The Second Test at Lord's Bradman declared a 'smasher', in a

July 1953 letter written from the Cumberland Hotel. He warned Rivett that his reports of the following Manchester and Leeds Tests were unlikely to be as good since matches as dramatic as that one were not common. He could not help quoting to Rivett the *Daily Mail* editor's appreciation of his Lord's reporting: 'May I just say how delighted I am with your splendid comments on this Test. You are more than fulfilling your part of the contract. You are giving us real substantial writing on the whole business of cricket which is so much more than just an account of play.'

Bradman quoted the praise not to big-note himself with his accomplished editor friend, but rather as an independent endorsement of the 'mental outlook' he had brought to the coverage and its merits over the standard fare: '. . . the sensation mongers amongst the sports writers are losing ground in this country all along the line and I am pleased to think the more sensible type of description is being so much appreciated.'

Problems arose again with the timing of cables. In a letter from the Midland Hotel in Manchester on 8 July 1953 Bradman responded to Rivett's concerns that copy destined for morning papers on Australia's east coast was not arriving fast enough. It was the *Daily Mail* letting down the side, he explained: the most recent copy that Rivett wanted filed by 9 am Wednesday morning had, in fact, been given to the *Daily Mail*'s Manchester office at 10 pm the previous night. Bradman still wasn't happy that filing at both ends of the day meant there could be no mention of last-minute happenings in the stories appearing in the east coast morning papers, but he emphasised his fulfilment of Rivett's remit nevertheless. 'Things are still going along well,' he told his editor, 'although I find it difficult to become accustomed to the noise and dirt of Manchester.'

Bradman's warning about future copy not living up to his Lord's stories proved prescient in Manchester – a 'dismal place', he opined, his spirit dampened, perhaps, by the showers and cold weather overwhelming the occasional fine day of that Coronation Year English summer. Writing from the Maynard Arms in Grindleford on 20 July 1953, Bradman said the cricket was so bad that even esteemed cricket writer Neville Cardus couldn't bring it alive.

Confusion arose at this time over an invitation Bradman received from an English publisher to turn his coverage of the 1953 tests for the *News* and *Daily Mail* into a book. He had earlier in the month flagged this possibility with Rivett. Things had not gone far down the track with the proposal and Bradman said he did not know, given his deal with News Limited, whether the copy could be used. Since it had already appeared in the newspaper Bradman thought it unlikely that such a book would be of concern to the company, but he expressly asked whether News Limited would give permission to reproduce the articles in book form.

Rivett must have reacted sharply. Bradman's reply politely thanked him for his comments – a mark of how early in their friendship these letters occur, since in later ones Bradman does not hesitate to go in hard when in his view Rivett got something badly wrong. But Bradman continued that Rivett may have 'misunderstood' the situation, and that the publisher concerned was not out to 'cash in unduly on anybody else' – that is, was not out to get a free ride on copyright material owned by News Limited. Bradman, in any case, was lukewarm about the idea 'when I cannot see any worthwhile financial result, nor can I visualise a book which would be satisfying either to myself or the public'. Bradman confirmed that his original arrangement with Rivett stood and that nothing would be done without News Limited's consent – and that, of course, had been the reason for his original inquiry.

Nearly a decade later, living in Zurich where he ran the International Press Institute, Rivett wrote admiringly of American press columnist Walter Lippmann to Bradman. In April 1962, Bradman sent his friend a copy of a column concerning Lippmann that he himself had come across. Rivett's belated response, after much intervening correspondence, suggests the column sent by Bradman was by William H. Chamberlain whom Rivett nailed in his reply as one of the 'great prostitutes' of journalism. 'I am always thankful that you have been so enormously successful at squash, sharebroking, golf and what the French call, le criquette,' Rivett warmed up in obviously over-the-top praise before going on to characterise Bradman as a plonker when it came to political analysis.

'He [Chamberlain], after being hired by William R. Hearst, that great suborner of American public opinion from 1895 to 1940, has become an hireling of the McCarthyist elements of the Roman Catholic church in the United States,' wrote Rivett. 'The doctrines of any influential political writer such as Lippmann are obviously anathema to these perverts. So they try a bit of character assassination. All over the world they find trusting business tycoons like Sir Donald Bradman, who fall for the guff. Nuff said'.

There was, of course, an element of the old bulls locking horns for a playful tussle over Lippmann. Bradman most likely sent the Chamberlain column on Lippmann as a provocation. Rivett makes this explicit in a postscript to his letter, saying he did not think that Bradman really agreed with Chamberlain but rather was designed to elicit Rivett's thunder: 'I can't bear to disappoint you . . .'

Rivett's call was correct. By return mail Bradman thanked him for his 'outburst' regarding Lippmann. 'Like most newspaper men of course you did not accurately read my letter,' wrote Bradman. 'I did not say I believed Chamberlain but of course you assumed it. Anyway after reading [Lippmann] and all the other "experts" I am never able to get any idea of what the future holds and I expect you to tell us in plain language . . .'

In the mid-1960s Rivett organised the commissioning of an article from Bradman which led to another amusing contretemps about the deal. Bradman sent off 'the Ford article' to Rivett and asked his view about whether it measured up. Rivett's subsequent note about compensation apparently amused Bradman. Bradman had not asked what the commission would pay and had not himself suggested a fee so legally, Bradman teased Rivett in reply, Rivett owed Bradman nothing and Bradman could sue Rivett for an undisclosed sum.

Negative, low grade journalism hurt cricket in the 1960s, Bradman believed, with the too frequent playing of the game feeding the problem. The plethora of cricket bred an air of familiarity – contempt, even – in the media, he told Rivett in 1964. Newspapers were too quick to condemn and slow to praise: 'cricket reporting today is tabloid – 6 or out'.

Double standards in reporting also worried Bradman. Critiques should be constructive, 'uplifting', he urged his friend, who had sent him a draft article for comment. Bradman told Rivett he could not go along with the knocking of the modern game. Rivett's disparagement of it drew Bradman's gentle ire. While there were elements of truth in Rivett's proposed article, his comparisons were not always fair: 'Every player in every era cannot be a Woolley or

Macartney.' Bradman urged his friend not to be despondent and, implicitly, not to be one of the ranks of journalistic knockers.

That the media had a duty to be constructive rather than corrosive was a persistent theme. Rivett's attempt to get Bradman to agree to a television interview marking his sixtieth birthday in 1968 caused Bradman to expound at length on what he considered to be the problem with the media.

Bradman told Rivett he was certain that a 'tycoon like Murdoch' had no interest in 'a small and insignificant figure' like him, or in the game. It could only be of interest to a Murdoch, he believed, insofar as it fitted in with the prevailing media pattern of bashing cricket. The Australian team had been given hell over the recent test by the press, he wrote, and public opinion in Australia keyed off their reports and commentary. While Bradman said he could talk to Rivett privately about such things, he argued it would be absurd to do so publicly.

'If I now went on the air & said Australia tried to win, I would be laughed at,' Bradman wrote. 'Nothing I could do or say could rectify the damage that the publicity has already done. And yet I *know* Australia desperately wanted to win, with the acknowledged proviso that if they couldn't win, they would try and avoid defeat.'

Bradman asked Rivett, the experienced media man, why it was that Australia and not England was attacked by the media. England's challenge in the recent Test was much easier than the one set Australia in 1948, when Australia pursued and gained victory despite the risks. Just before tea he had thought England had the game in its grasp, 'but she put up the shutters, *with 6 wkts in hand*, & *we* get blamed'.

In his view there was little hope of him influencing the media when journalists were bent on reporting facts which were actually opinion – the opinions, quite often, of reporters who had never played cricket and were ignorant of its laws and lore. With some of the reporters sent out to cover tests it was the equivalent of sending him, Bradman, to cover a medical congress in Salzburg on the technical aspects of immunisation. 'Shades of Arthur Calwell,' he quipped. 'I am an idealist & in particular I feel the press, with its monopolistic control, has a bounded duty to preserve, uplift & encourage the features of humanity which are good,' Bradman told Rivett. This conflicted, he realised, with the news sense of an editor who believed that semi-naked page three pics would sell more papers than stories about cricket's character-building nature: 'He is right of course – in terms of circulation – both sales & blood – but history may yet record why the present civilisation decayed & fell – and it won't be because we played cricket.'

Bradman's jaundice about the media grew as the years went on. So much in the press was biased, distorted, half true or 'economic rubbish' that one lost interest under the mental fatigue of it all, he told Rivett in 1971. News coverage the following year of son John's decision to change his name to 'Bradsen' triggered further devastating accusations of calculated cruelty by the media.

Wearing, too, were the cheap shots by ignorant reporters over things some people might dismiss as inconsequential. Bradman recounted to Rivett how a television commentator interviewing Ken Cunningham, who had been omitted from the test team, asked what one had to do to get selected: lunch with Bradman at the Adelaide Club? Bradman was neither a selector at the time nor a member of the Adelaide Club: 'All he wanted was to stir up filth.'

It kept up, year in, year out. Wearily, he responded to Rivett's comments about an article which appeared in the Melbourne press: 'Yes, I'm still bread & jam to the press . . .' Bradman joked that if Gough Whitlam lasted much longer in office, everyone would be broke including the newspapers and television stations. 'At least I'm enjoying Alan Reid on Sunday nights,' he wrote of the long-time Canberra press gallery journalist and political insider.

Even with media engagements likely to be sympathetic, Bradman was apprehensive. In April 1974 Rivett told Bradman how much he had enjoyed Ashley Mallet's interview with Don – conducted hurriedly, Bradman replied, before Mallet's departure for New Zealand. He was relieved at Rivett's assessment: 'I confess I was a little dubious.'

Bradman was bemused by the Australian Journalists Association (AJA), which he believed asserted on behalf of its members the freedom to write what they liked, when they wanted. Rivett was probably an 'AJA man', Bradman guessed, but he doubted his friend would support East Africans, Sri Lankans, West Indians, Australians and others 'having open slather to attack the umpires, opposing players etc (doubtless through a ghost) at close of play each day'. That would make a real contribution to international harmony, he quipped, 'like hell'.

Rivett still occasionally tried to tempt Bradman into media lairs, inviting him in June 1975 to address a press luncheon that would also be attended by luminaries in other fields. Bradman regrettably declined – 'much as I would like to be in the company of Glenda Jackson (some of the others doubtful)' – explaining that health problems had led him to give up public speaking.

Bradman's take on press perniciousness was evident in an experience concerning a couple living rough but happy on John's farm, related to Rivett as a story where the media did more harm than good. The *Sunday Mail* discovered the couple living in the leaky, bathroomless farmhouse, washing their clothes in the creek, and published an exposé. The local council's arrival the next day led to the house being condemned and the couple expelled. They had been 'really deliriously happy, growing vegetables, getting away from the world' and living rent free, Bradman told Rivett. They were forced to leave, with nowhere to go, and were now presumably paying rent somewhere. Squatters had subsequently moved into the farmhouse, having to be ejected by the police. Instead of being tended by caring inhabitants, the farmhouse would travel the sad path to weed infestation, ruin and fire hazard. 'Great world,' he wrote. 'I hope the news-hound who wrote the story has a conscience because of the misery he created for others.'

Bradman assumed that Rivett continued to defend the freedom of the press. For readers, he argued, the issue was different. 'The problem is to know whether what one reads is true or not,' wrote Bradman, 'and I fear that applies to all press anywhere in the world.'

6 *Family & Friends*

'Life seems to get busier and busier. One wonders where the time goes and what one achieves. Or am I getting old and imagining things[?]'
— Don Bradman

'Love from all five [Rivetts] to all Bradmans,
As ever, mate . . .'
— Rohan Rivett

Twin concerns about the incredible demands on Bradman's time and concern about the health and welfare of the family feature constantly in the letters Bradman wrote Rivett. The first extensive letter mostly concerned practical matters to do with Bradman's coverage of the 1953 Test series in England for the *News*. But at the close Bradman outlines the inundation of requests to play in Sunday cricket matches in England, open fetes and give speeches which, on top of the demands of his voluminous correspondence and calls on old friends, made the days pass so very quickly. Still, he and Jessie were enjoying themselves and were in good health.

The Bradmans' two children, John and Shirley, then fourteen and twelve respectively, had been left in Adelaide during the 1953 trip. Bradman passed on Jessie's gratitude for a cable from Rivett which reported on the children's well-being. They had been so worried about John, Bradman wrote, and they were relieved that he had not suffered a recurrence of his 'old trouble'. John contracted polio as a boy. Shirley had an intellectual disability. Deep feelings for and concern about the children – especially John, whose problematic relationship with his father emerges strongly as the correspondence goes on – form a continuing, poignant thread in the exchange. Despite her obvious challenges, Shirley seemed a joy to Bradman, who loved her vim for life. Rivett was obviously one of the few – perhaps the only – person with whom Bradman fully unburdened his anxieties, safe in the knowledge that Rivett could be trusted.

The word 'mate' is rarely in Bradman's own letters. One of the three occasions it is used is in an enigmatic note on the letterhead of Melbourne's Hotel Windsor. It says simply: 'Thanks mate. You're a Pal.' There is a postscript that tells Rivett that he, Bradman, was not as obstinate as Lawry. But the reason for the note and the circumstances of its writing are not known. On another occasion it is used sarcastically in a Bradman onslaught about a cricket piece Rivett had published which had offended him on multiple fronts. The handle typically used by Australian men for each other appeared not to be for The Don.

The commonplace matters that provided the filler in friendship have their place in the Bradman letters alongside the extensive cricket dialogue, investment analysis, political commentary and family concerns. In April 1962, with the Rivetts living in Switzerland because of Rohan's work with the International Press Institute, Bradman did not skimp in his coverage of parochial football triumphs or the weather. He was buoyed up by South Australian National Football League team Norwood's great start to the season, beating West Adelaide, the previous year's premiers, and then thrashing Port

Adelaide on Anzac Day kicking 10 goals in the final quarter. Rohan had the best of the weather, however, in Bradman's view. Despite being midway through autumn, Adelaide suffered a 'stinking dust storm' on the day of writing, and was 86 degrees Fahrenheit (30 degrees Celsius) – 'the worst April day I remember'.

The weather had been hot and dry for some time and Bradman, who had a modest farm in the Adelaide hills, feared severe drought was imminent. The tenant on their farm had been breaking wild horses, and John Bradman, now twenty-three, was about to join him; Jessie and Shirley enjoyed the Easter Monday horseracing at Oakbank; and Don was about to join battle as part of Kooyonga Golf Club's Simpson Cup side. Some Zurich snow would be welcome Adelaide way, he quipped.

In June 1962 Jessie and Shirley took a Pacific cruise, stopping at Fiji. Bradman apologised that the 'cooking etc' he had been doing in their absence made him tardy in replying to Rivett's interesting missives. Great news from the Bradmans' perspective was an impending visit by the Rivetts to South Australia in September. Rohan proposed they get together at the Rivetts' Fleurieu Peninsula cottage in Port Willunga on 7 or 8 September, in the exquisite McLaren Vale winemaking district. 'Am completely silent about your movements,' Bradman assured Rivett, who dreaded being besieged by Adelaide acquaintances during his brief visits to the state. 'It will be some concession to be able to talk to you & more so to talk to Nan . . .'

Bradman reeled off his 'usual crop of deaths', naming five people who had recently died before proceeding to announce that Victoria had 'killed' Western Australia in the interstate football struggle and that, despite the fact that South Australia had previously beaten Western Australia by 32 points, the consensus was that 'Vic will kill SA'. This was the usual fare for Australian Rules football, in which Victoria was dominant, but what came next seemed to surprise Bradman as much as it would have Rivett: 'Old Don Bradman has been selected in the practice squad for S.A. at *golf*. A real Ripley story.'

As often became the case, Bradman confided the worrying aspects of his family life to Rivett. In June 1962 it was son John's knee, likely in need of an operation, the only bright part of which he said would be a few weeks' respite from John's tuba playing. 'Our love to Nan and the children,' was the warm farewell, along with a reminder of how much they looked forward to getting together at Port Willunga.

In a long reply written in July from the Montreaux Palace Hotel in Switzerland, Rivett wished for better news on John's knee. He and Nan had booked their sons David and Keith into Canberra Boys Grammar School, he wrote, impressed by the then headmaster and former New South Wales rugby champion P.J. McKeown. Rivett had been conducting a workshop on nuclear disarmament in Montreaux, prior to travelling on to Paris and London in August 1962, and then on through Asia for the visit home to Australia.

Expeditions by the Rivetts come up often and, nearly as often, the travels of Jessie and Shirley Bradman as well. A letter the following year, in May 1963, contains Bradman's heartfelt approval that the Rivetts were enjoying the beauty of France. 'And I love the Citroen car,' he said. 'If only it looked as nice as it really is.' Jessie was in Alice Springs while he was at home in Adelaide grappling with his workload, cricket-related and otherwise.

Bradman's letter to Rivett in July 1963 showed him flat out, and deeply engaged in business matters. Bradman was so stretched, in fact, that he would move straight on to the matter of Rivett's share portfolio from pressure of time. He nevertheless managed to sandwich a crack and a compliment into the intense investment commentary that forms the body of the letter. 'Gosh I hope your typewriter turns up soon,' Bradman stirred. 'Not that I mind trying to decipher your letters. They are a better mental exercise than a X-word puzzle but they certainly consume time.' At the end came the salve. 'Don't know that I have helped much,' Bradman said of his own extraordinarily detailed stockmarket advice to Rivett, 'but then I never had a brain like yours which does a week's work in a day.'

The Rivetts were shortly to repatriate from Zurich, via London and Nairobi, to Melbourne where they would settle in Camberwell. The transition was to occur between September and December 1963. Rivett wanted freedom from money worries during the family's re-establishment in Australia. The 1961 credit squeeze induced by the Menzies Government a couple of years earlier to slow down the overheated Australian economy had hit many people hard, including the Rivetts. It was Bradman to whom Rivett turned for advice on whether or not he should cash out some of his seventy thousand pound share portfolio, putting the proceeds into fixed interest investments. 'Yours of 30/7 couldn't have been saner or more helpful,' Rivett wrote. 'If you feel that's enough for one customer, I understand. But, like everybody who has been bitten hard a couple of times by being greedy I don't want to be caught napping this time when the inevitable turn of the tide comes and that's why I've belabored you with this.'

'Fancy having to answer your letter on my birthday instead of playing golf,' Bradman wrote back on 27 August. 'Oh well – it does my conscience good to think I am trying to help someone – even if I fail.' Bradman advised his friend carefully, putting the focus on the net rather than headline effect of Rivett's choices. He advised 'moderate compromise' rather than either alternative. It was steadying advice for a man on the other side of the globe worried about the immediate future for himself and his family. Posed Bradman: 'Have I been helpful? I doubt it.' But from Rivett's point of view Bradman's investment counsel was both valuable and a comfort.

When the tables were turned and it was Bradman who was troubled, it was Rivett to whom he turned. The death of close stockbroker friend Len Bullock in February 1964 was such a time. Bradman was godfather to their son Ian. Bullock and his wife, Margaret, had a car accident near the South Australian river town of Murray Bridge on the return trip from Geelong College in Victoria, where they had just taken Ian, a boarder. Bullock's death left no room for thoughts of shares, he apologised to Rivett. It had triggered something of a personal crisis.

Bullock had bequeathed Bradman the goodwill of his stockbroking firm, but the will had been drawn up before Bullock had taken on a partner, Bob Pentelow. The legal and accounting problems posed by this were immense and Bradman said he was immersed in continuous conferences about what to do. It was questionable whether he could or should accept the inheritance, he confided in Rivett, which was more a liability than an asset unless he chose to 'buck in and work like hell again'. Pentelow wanted him back in the firm, but Bradman was now fifty-five years old. 'Would I kill myself if I went back?' Bradman asked Rivett. 'What about my Coy Directorships? Would I have to give up cricket administration?'

John Bradman's future figured heavily as Bradman wrestled with the question: 'John is really the big problem because I want to assure his future if I can.' Concern about his son, now in his mid-twenties but still living at home and unsettled about his direction, was a regular thread in the correspondence. Bradman wished Rivett was with him so he could draw on his mind, 'so much more fertile than mine'. He would get the best advice he could and decide alone, he told his friend, and stand or fall by the decision.

Rivett offered counsel by return mail but in late February Bradman replied that he had 'wrestled incessantly' with the problem, still without result. For his own part he would rather not get directly involved again in the firm, but 'for John's sake' he said he must give it his full consideration: 'Frankly my main worry is whether I could now stand up to the volume & intensity of the work.'

Jessie and Shirley and possibly John would go to England for the cricket, but he could not, Bradman wrote, declining Rivett's invitation to attend the Trent Bridge test together. The Australian team would be staying at the Black Boy Hotel in Nottingham itself, which he did not recommend, but as to better alternatives he could not help Rivett out.

The situation triggered by Len Bullock's death was resolved by early March. In a postscript to his late February letter, which Bradman was tardy in posting, he told Rivett he had decided not to return to the firm but would maintain a relationship with Bob Pentelow of the kind he had enjoyed with Len Bullock – a professional association but not a structural involvement in the firm. 'There will be a place for John later,' he added.

Bradman told Rivett he would save the details until the families came together at Easter for dinner at their Kensington home. 'I have a bottle of very good red,' he wrote. 'Will you let me know if we can expect you?' John Bradman's future had, for the time being, been sorted out, at least from his father's point of view. Rivett had posed in his previous letter whether some mixed farming might be the answer to John's unresolved career question. That was out, replied Bradman: John would have to equip himself to be a stockbroker and that required his undivided attention.

Despite childhood polio, John Bradman was a talented athlete who had attended Adelaide's elite private school St Peters. He was a good cricketer, playing for the local team, Kensington, for which his father had also played. However, the crushing media pressure triggered by The Don's fame cruelled the experience for the young John, who gave cricket away despite his promise. Athletics engaged him for some time. He was a talented hurdler who had legitimate hopes for Olympic selection in his early twenties. The picture emerges in his father's letters to Rivett of a somewhat diffident young man struggling to work out his life's plan, prone to the blues for long periods – a source of deep worry for his parents.

The impending 1964 Ashes series lifted spirits all round. Jessie, Shirley and John were getting excited in the run-up to their departure from Adelaide, Bradman wrote in April. He returned a cheque to Rivett, who had written asking Bradman to buy tickets for the Lord's Test for him through the MCC. Instead Bradman offered to fix him up with a daily pair of seats courtesy of Australia's High Commissioner to London, Sir Eric Harrison. Harrison undertook to set them aside from the two hundred seats allocated to visiting Australians by ballot through the High Commission for Lord's – an offer Rivett did not take up.

The excitement helped offset the health woes which had struck Jessie and Don. Treatment for a separate health problem had caused Jessie's rheumatic condition to flare up, and Bradman was in a worse state. 'Poor old dad (that is me) is very despondent because I've had a foul attack of fibrositis for just on a month and can't shift it,' he wrote. It was a recurrence of a problem whose origin lay in Bradman's playing days. His back, shoulder and arm were all affected and he was in extreme pain, unable even to play golf. 'We are a poor lot, but don't let me dwell on our infirmities,' he told Rivett. 'At least we are alive.'

Rivett in reply disclosed his own health worries, and Bradman said he was not surprised – that for years he and Jessie had counselled Rohan to take things easier rather than living like a 'human dynamo' of inexhaustible energy: 'I, too, had a similar idea once but found out, like everyone else who has tried it, I was wrong.' This realisation hurt the ego, he wrote, and some people put the resulting change down to laziness. 'But in the end,' he wrote, 'it boils down to what you want or expect from life and how long you would like it to last.' He passed on John Bradman's observation, on visiting the Rivetts in Melbourne with his mother and sister en route for England, that Rohan was now quieter and more thoughtful, living at sixty miles per hour rather than the previous ninety. 'As for Nan,' Bradman wrote, 'he has fallen for her and [thinks] she is beaut.' Bradman declined Rivett's invitation to visit while the family was in England. His back was worse and the next trip would be to the specialist for x-rays.

Work on the land provided one route for physical regeneration once the worst of a fibrositis episode had passed. As the 1960s wore on, the Bradmans' small farm was absorbing more of Don's energy and interest than it had previously. Woodchopping, or axemanship as he called it, had become a specialty, despite it not being a spectator sport, he quipped. 'So in my lonely exclusion I enjoy the ring of steel on wood & get the thrill of a forester in a fine clean cut,' Bradman wrote to Rivett. 'And it has put 30 yards on my golf drive for sure. I am meeting the challenge of the land with fortitude. Other people have a different name for it but I can afford to pity their ignorance & go on revelling in my joust with nature.'

Yet an air of philosophical resignation in the face of growing age and increasing political uncertainty began to dot the correspondence. Bradman reeled off recent departures from the world stage: Nehru, Kennedy, Macmillan. At home Menzies was getting old. 'All in all an uncertain outlook,' he wrote, 'which you & I can't change so mate take it easy – don't kill yourself chasing rainbows – & let your wife have your companionship as long as possible on this earth.'

Sometimes it was almost all gloom. One letter reeled off a list of dead, dying and ill friends and associates. Bradman told Rohan he had himself just endured five really bad days with an infection and bad back but was now all right. Not so a Mrs Dunham, an acquaintance of the Bradmans whom Rivett had recently met. Mrs Dunham had resigned from her position at a Melbourne hospital, moved back to Adelaide and was dead within the fortnight. Her nineteen year old son 'is left all alone in the world', Bradman, who was executor of her will, told Rivett. He recounted visiting his great friend T.H. 'Brock' Brown who was slipping away in Adelaide's Calvary Hospital – 'heart rending'. Another friend had been diagnosed with throat cancer. But even as he sombrely went through the list, some levity was injected: 'It may be callous to add Vic. beat us at footy, Sturts beat Norwood, and I failed to qualify yesterday in the Kooyonga Golf Championships.' Nor did he let the gloomy hospital list nix his chance to gloat over those likely to be miffed by a recently announced imperial honours list. There must have been broken hearts when only Dr Leonard Lindon got a knighthood, he said: 'No Turner – Young – Lodge or Carter to say nothing about all the other triers.'

The health woes continued. Bradman's back pain was so bad in September 1964 that instead of going to see a good movie as planned, he stayed home and wrote to Rivett. It was 'this old war time back trouble', Bradman said – displaced discs – and his Sydney doctor wanted to have him hospitalised and encased in plaster straight away. But Bradman resisted in favour of osteopathic treatment which had fixed him before, in case he could head off the 'humiliating immobility' of the other approach: 'It's getting me down a bit I must admit but that's enough about my troubles.' He spent a couple of hours considering Rivett's portfolio and came up with three single-spaced typed pages of investment analysis to send to his friend.

Mercifully, Rivett's reply was typed. 'It makes such a difference,' jabbed Bradman, 'when I can read and digest your letters in minutes instead of hours.' His gratitude for this spilled over into graciousness about Rivett's observations of the Australian cricket team just chosen by the selectors, including Bradman.

In fact, Bradman was in a weakened state. Jessie and the family were away and he was fending for himself, losing much condition in the process – grief about the Manchester test perhaps contributing, he mused. Anticipating the family's return he was busy decorating the inside of their home at Kensington and trying to rebuild his health.

There was a deep sense of love and duty in Bradman's responsiveness to Rivett's missives. One four-page letter written in 1964 came from a 'dog tired' Bradman who had driven five hundred miles earlier in the week and was weighed down by problems on multiple fronts – 'especially John – no nearer solution, but one must keep trying'. Despite this Bradman picked up the pen and responded to Rivett's investment queries and wrote a long critique of a draft article on cricket matters he had sent: 'Suppose I should answer your letter as best I can in case you want to publish something or buy or sell something, so for what it is worth – here goes.'

Rivett responded in kind. He was especially supportive of Bradman through his and Jessie's travails with John Bradman's apparent prolonged depression. 'I've never been up against a problem like this before,' Bradman confided, thanking Rivett for his kind words about John. He thanked him, too, for Rivett's proposals about options for John, but said that at that moment he was unlikely to do anything but stay put. John would not let him and Jessie make a decision about John's future direction in life, Bradman wrote, nor did he seem capable of making a decision of his own: 'However it is our personal problem & we'll do our best to solve it though I fear it will be a long & hard road.' Shirley was getting on with things, on the other hand, and was moving into a flat the following week. Bradman's family issues did not make him grudging in praise for the Rivetts' own brood. He said he was glad they had done well in their exams. Rivett was lucky to have such smart children – they would be able to keep him, he said, when Rivett was old.

Yet some quiet playfulness from The Don was rarely far away. There was light relief from him in January 1965 during a difficult visit from his mother-in-law, whom he described to Rivett as 'quite a handful'. He reminded Rohan of earlier correspondence in which Rivett had named his preferred Australian team for the imminent series against the West Indies. 'Ex profundis ad astra', declared Bradman by way of comment. 'I haven't the faintest idea what that means, but it is what you added at the end, so I guess it means E&OE.'

In March Bradman and Jessie were going for a few days rest at the Peninsula Golf Club in Frankston, Victoria. Would Rohan and Nan join them there for dinner one evening, he asked. Rivett would have to dig out his dinner suit – 'very posh down there' – but Bradman guessed that he could still fit into it. Rivett had regained his punch, Bradman judged from his friend's most recent letters: the 'pithy, racy style of giving orders, asking questions and interweaving questions on cricket were right back to the form of "why do you read the bloody Bully".'

The Frankston sojourn had done the trick, Bradman wrote to Rivett in late March. They were feeling better except for Jessie's knee, which was giving her trouble. The only remedy was a week in bed for which Jessie's on-the-go nature did not allow. She was about to run the garden stall for the Ashford fete as well as selling badges for the charity which helped children with intellectual disabilities.

Rivett had made further suggestions during March about career options for John. Bradman thanked him but, after much thought, decided the practical difficulties surrounding them could not be overcome. 'Frankly I think it would do him the world of good to get a job elsewhere & to live away from home,' he wrote. 'But he has got himself into a state where he refuses to accept this. He feels utterly dependent on us.' John was convinced, his father said, that the attainment of some professional status – as a dentist, for example – was the way forward. This meant matriculating to university and Bradman felt that if this was the route John wanted to take, matriculation would be easier to attempt while living at home with them in Kensington. John was having a go already, trying to do Maths 1 and Maths 2, but found it difficult. John's work habits were poor, Bradman said; moreover John had never had much flair for subjects such as this and absorbing the theorems seemed beyond him. Bradman tried to buoy his son up saying that, after several years break from study, it would get easier as he went along.

Bradman and Jessie were struggling to deal with the conflicting emotional problems of getting John through what they saw as a critical period. In their view, it could make or break his future. They were perpetually torn 'between the desireable & the achievable and there is so much scope for error'. Bradman told Rivett how kind it was of him to take an interest but that they did not want to burden him with the family's problems: 'John really is a wonderful lad & to see him so confused & torn isn't at all comforting. And the problems are not of his own making. Such is life.'

A week later the word on John was no better. Things were worse, in fact, he told Rivett. John's self-confidence was terrible, Bradman wrote, saying he felt 'so sorry for the poor kid'. He and Jessie had a long battle ahead to get John set but it must be their number one priority – a bit late in life for them to have to face such problems, he said resignedly, but it was all relative: 'Somehow I have always found it the hardest job to cope with family emotional matters. Straight forward business or matters involving outsiders are much easier.' He envied Rivett's forthcoming trip to the West Indies.

A quick note to Rivett on business issues the next day saw Bradman report a further slide in John's situation: 'His outlook couldn't be lower and it is a real problem.' Bradman had asked John whether he would like to go to the West Indies with Rivett. John's eyes had brightened, but he had then declined the offer, saying he could not enjoy the trip since it would waste time and lead nowhere. Yet when pressed about where he wanted to get to, John could only say that he did not know.

During Rivett's trip to the West Indies, Bradman corresponded with Nan Rivett, who shared the letters with Rohan on his return. At the end of June Rivett wrote to Bradman about the cricket, about 'Ming' and about his letters to Nan. Bradman thrived on Rivett's discourse which 'enlightened, amused and entertained' him. Bradman wanted more. What about dinner, he asked, at the Rivetts' Port Willunga house during their spring visit from Melbourne?

Bradman seemed brighter. While John remained 'enigmatic and difficult', they took comfort from the fact that his state had stabilised, although Bradman was knocking himself out on the family's small farm with its fifty sheep. It was doing him good, he thought, though that conclusion was hard to accept at night when he got muscle cramps 'or when I am on the 1st tee and can't swing the club as fast as Lloyd Dumas' (the chairman of Advertiser Newspapers Limited and a pillar of the Adelaide establishment).

More work for 'poor old D.G.B' was in prospect, too, with the likelihood that the incumbent president of the South Australian Cricket Association (SACA) would resign in a few months' time. But he was thinking of selling his seat on the Adelaide Stock Exchange: 'John, being as he is, I see no point in carrying on.'

This triggered a round of joshing between the two. Rivett guessed that, at fifty-seven years old, Bradman might be 'young' enough to be president of the SACA and that he was rich enough to be able to slough off his stock exchange seat. Bradman answered in mock outrage about his endless need to correct Rivett – that he was, in fact, '*old* enough' to be SACA president. But there was melancholy in his response to the stock exchange jibe. Reduced business from clients going overseas and lower rates of commission meant he couldn't afford the fees to remain a member, he said. It was sad, he said, but the materialistic world must be faced. The prospect of a free meal and a drink with the Rivetts in September was cheering against this gloom.

'I've been working like a bloody navvy on the farm,' Bradman wrote. 'It would have killed a normal man. In my case it has cured my aches & pains, restored my flagging muscles & I feel pretty fit again. In fact I think I'm fitter than at any time since 1938.' This was against the backdrop of reminders of mortality like the death of Jessie's eighty-seven year old mother the previous week – ultimately a blessing, he said.

Rivett wrote back with sad news of their own elderly family members, and Bradman sympathised. 'But that is life & we can't avoid our responsibilities,' he added. With the passing of Jessie's mother, all four of their parents had gone. Jessie had managed to go to Melbourne to see her mother before the end, but that had caused its own problems. She fell and broke her wrist in two places at the airport when caught in a tangle with a young mother who crossed Jessie's path chasing her errant child with a pusher. Jessie had tripped on a wheel and fell heavily on the tiled airport floor. Bradman would not be around to help Jessie for long on her return from Melbourne because he had the annual 'wake' of one of his boards in Sydney to attend. Things would be hectic for the next six months but somehow, somewhere over the summer, Bradman told him, they would get together.

Bradman spent a week in Sydney which was drenched with rain. Adelaide desperately needed the same, he said. Awareness of South Australia's dryness, the perpetual experience of or flirtation with drought, dotted the correspondence. Bradman had been even more worried upon hearing of three men dying in a ruckus at a Melbourne football game, concerned Rivett could be one of them. All was well once he realised his friend supported neither team and was unlikely to have been there. 'Sturt killed Norwood here – poor little Shirley was nearly in tears,' he wrote. 'She loves Norwood, but even her blue dress and red jumper brought them no luck.'

Jessie's wrist was improving, Bradman told Rivett in late September 1965. She had lit a fire on the farm and within minutes the fire brigade had to be called because it looked like Mount Lofty might go up: 'Life is never dull.'

Getting together with Rivett was always desired but all too rarely possible. In October 1965 Bradman responded with an outline of his horror schedule to Rivett's news that a visit might be imminent. Bradman would leave on Thursday for a week in Perth, he said, followed by commitments relating to visits to Adelaide by the

Victorian cricket team and the MCC in succession. They would need to talk on the phone to marry their arrangements. Bradman sent warm wishes, as usual, to Nan and the children. 'Our picture is unchanged – worrying and unpredictable – but one can do no more than live on from day to day,' Bradman confided.

Despite his frenetic schedule, there are glimpses of a solitary man who sometimes crossed the line into loneliness. 'It was like a breath of fresh air to get your letter,' he wrote to Rivett in November 1965, 'because for once you had time to relapse into personal meanderings. Even if it was 6am it was worth it from my point of view.'

Among other things, Rivett had given Bradman a rundown on the three Rivett children. Bradman said he wished he could find something similar to say about John instead of more of the same despondency that had plagued him for so long. It was the most baffling problem he had faced all his life, Bradman told his friend. 'It is so frustrating and wearing,' he told Rivett. 'He cannot share the burden with others nor shelve it. At times I despair, but we must carry on & pray that somehow, someday, things will be brighter. Perhaps I'll see you during one of the tests & unburden a bit more.'

Rumination about old age also crept in to the reflections. One could not look forward to old age with any pleasure, Bradman wrote, but there was a quiet fatalism and resignation that went along with aging. In becoming attuned to being old, one's thoughts and outlook were very different from those one had at thirty. Bradman told Rivett that he accepted things then, as a fifty-seven year old, that he would not have tolerated even a decade before. On the other hand, some irritations were eternal: 'I hate making speeches & get infuriated when I feel I've made a bad one & people insist on telling me it was good.' Amidst the irritations, however, there were some new satisfactions, too. The presidency of the SACA was one which, while creating a lot more work for him, seemed to be appreciated.

The sheep, some twenty-seven of them in that spring of 1965, also demanded attention. He told Rivett the farm was overrun with huge, poisonous brown snakes confronting him at every turn. John had killed two of them, he said, and Jessie had got caught up with another. Bradman never went anywhere on the farm without the then recommended kit for snakebite – a tourniquet, razor blade and Condy's crystals – in his hip pocket for quick action: 'By the grace of God I hope they remain there.'

During the Sydney Ashes Test in January 1966, Bradman had tried without success to contact Rivett. Perhaps his friend was as low as Bradman was about the cricket and couldn't face him, he mused in a letter to Rivett afterwards. Bradman was already back in Adelaide; the family were on their way back, by car.

A disastrous sight awaited him. A water pipe in their Kensington home had burst in their absence causing major damage: the walls and carpets as well as the ceilings were ruined. The house had to be completely rewired. Bradman told Rivett he was navigating the house with a torch, avoiding holes in the floor where repairs were being made. Miraculously no-one was electrocuted and the mess had been discovered in the nick of time, just heading off an electrical fire which would have destroyed the house altogether. 'All this with a test ahead & visitors coming,' Bradman despaired. 'When poor Jessie sees it she will cry.' Bradman's work renovating the house during Jessie's most recent trip to England had been wrecked. In the argot of the time, Bradman told Rivett he must have 'killed a Chinaman somewhere'. He would tell Rivett more when he went to Melbourne for the Fifth Test, he said.

A major development for the Bradman family occurred in 1966 when John took up university studies in Adelaide, but no sooner had he started than medical misfortune struck. John had successive skin cancers burnt off one ear. The ear subsequently became infected with a rare bacterium for which only a couple of modern drugs were effective. His ear swelled to huge proportions and oozed pus, Bradman told Rivett. On top of the pain, it interrupted John's university studies right at the outset when he was so keen and had so much work to do – but the worst was over, Bradman said, and things would now improve.

'I haven't been too good myself – very tired & over worked, & the doctor wants me to break it down which I must do,' he wrote. At least the house disaster was virtually fixed: the remaining furniture would be moved back in the next day, ten weeks after Bradman had first returned to the massive mess. Later in April he and Jessie intended going to Frankston for some golf and relaxation. The trip would enable him to try out his new Valiant which just that week had superseded his Hawk.

After the Frankston retreat, Don and Jessie had a 'stinking hot' trip home to Adelaide with a problem front wheel that made them lucky to reach Kensington at all. But 'we did, and a charming letter from you was a most pleasant antidote to the pile of bills'. Bradman told Rivett he had not realised how tired he was until he reached Frankston: with only two days' relaxation there he was still exhausted and had returned to Adelaide feeling very flat. He had to cut back on his commitments.

'Forty years of limelight and constant recognition must have taken a heavy toll of my nervous energy though one hates to admit it,' he wrote. 'A fortnight in Paris or Rome would be a God-send.' Bradman thanked Rivett for all his kindness, and empathised with Rivett's fortunately relatively minor domestic worries. The horizon was bright for Rohan and Nan, though, he emphasised. Bradman contrasted the Rivetts' situation with friends of his and Jessie's, both sixty years old, whose daughter had just abandoned three small children and a migrant husband who had no family in Australia. At this advanced age they now faced raising another young family: their grandchildren.

John Bradman's mood continued to be a drag on the Bradman household, however, and Rivett continued offering insights and advice on the tender subject. Bradman thanked him but said John was their problem, and he and Jessie must face it and deal with it to the best of their ability. 'Your thoughts & goodwill are a comfort & one never knows what is ahead but basically the only person who can win this battle is John himself,' Bradman wrote. 'We can help & befriend but somehow we can't bully & we believe time will solve it.' Lying ill in bed with the 'flu, he still managed to reach out for the positive, telling Rivett that 'as usual we shall pass out into sunshine' no matter how long and bumpy the road ahead appeared to be. Shirley Bradman, despite her intellectual disability, seemed to induce much less anxiety in Bradman. After a period of living independently, she had just been rushed off to hospital for an emergency appendectomy, and was now living back home with him and Jessie until stronger, but was otherwise fine. It was bad timing since Shirley was due to be measured up for a bridesmaid's dress for the wedding the following week of her best friend, Barby Williss.

In the meantime Bradman worked on a speech to give at a dinner celebrating Victor Richardson's cricketing career. 'If only I could speak like you,' he told Rivett, 'with your flair & confidence. But somehow my inferiority complex reaches its zenith in speeches.' Jessie was going well despite recent travails, he reported. Bradman sent his love to 'Rivett's beautiful wife' and his 'salaams' to the Rivett children.

Bradman did not conceal his soft spot for Nan Rivett. 'Firstly dealing with Nan's P.S.,' he began a letter to Rohan in August 1966. 'Why "Big love" to the others and only a slice for me? What about reversing it?' Rohan had reported in his previous letter that he and Nan had been in North Queensland on a lecture tour. Bradman said in reply that he would have given anything to hear Nan; no doubt others were happy just to have heard Rohan, he teased.

A show on sporting greats including Bradman, Dawn Fraser and Betty Cuthbert had recently appeared on television, and Rohan wanted to know when Bradman's story in its complete form would be told. 'It already has,' Bradman replied, 'up to 1948 – and that will be the end.' There was no later footage than that because, as the program's producers had found after searching the world, there was no footage to be had beyond that time. A contemporary interview with Bradman had been shot in Adelaide and cut into the program for broadcast. 'Had I known Betty & Dawn were going to be there I would have journeyed to Melbourne for a night out with them,' he wrote. 'But as usual I missed all the fun.'

Fun, of which Don and Jessie clearly found the Rivetts an enormous source, was in short supply in the Bradman household. The prospect of John's mood deteriorating again hung like a pall over Bradman. 'This malaise is the supreme tragedy of my life for

I seem so powerless to help,' Bradman confided. 'I can only trust in divine providence that in the end there will be a light at the end of the road.'

Bradman swore Rohan and Nan to secrecy about the break-up of a significant relationship of John's: his Scandinavian girlfriend, much loved by Don and Jessie, was going home as the match had not taken. There was no use interfering or asking about it, but Bradman felt that John could search the world and not find another young woman so wonderful. 'But there you are,' he wrote. 'I hope to goodness there won't be another of these dreadful depressions when she goes but he will miss her more than he realises.' John's copious university work could be the salvation, Bradman mused: it might keep his mind on track. 'You appreciate what a difficult and harrowing time we have had with John . . .' he told Rivett. 'Somehow I can't seem to find out what makes John tick and what makes him come unstuck.'

Bradman's salvation was the physical work he did on their small farm. He had been putting in every spare moment there and felt better for it. His physical restoration was such that he had even won the Kooyonga Golf Club captain's trophy, beating the club champion 7/6 over 36 holes.

As 1966 drew to a close Bradman wrote to Rivett that he hoped the year's end would see them get together. All was well their end, he reported. As often seemed to be the case, however, the Bradmans and Rivetts were set to pass like ships in the night unless Rohan, on the day he was due to arrive for an Adelaide visit on 27 December, wanted to come to the closing day of the South Australia v Queensland Shield match as Bradman's guest. He and Jessie were leaving for interstate at dawn the next day.

Rivett had mentioned the Meckiff–Simpson case in his most recent letter, which saw Australian bowler Ian Meckiff sue cricketer Bobby Simpson for defamation over Simpson's allegation that Meckiff was a 'chucker'. Bradman said it had raised a smile: it could even be better than Playford v Rivett, raising the charges of seditious libel Rivett had faced over the Rupert Max Stuart affair. 'All I hope is that I don't get dragged into the stupid affair,' Bradman wrote. 'They must both be off their rockers.' Bradman concluded with love to the family: 'Hope the nips did well in the Exams.'

With 1967 came better prospects for Don, Jessie, Rohan and Nan to get together. The Rivetts planned a mid-year break in Port Willunga. The Bradmans planned an early May visit to Frankston for some rest and recreation at the Peninsula Golf Club. Could the Rivetts join them for dinner, Don wanted to know: 'As usual it is a black tie affair (relic of the Commonwealth) but I'm sure you wouldn't mind that to have a free dinner with the Bradmans.' In the return mail the Rivetts pressed Don and Jessie to attend a social engagement at the Rivetts' home in Melbourne during the Frankston stay. The invitation was so insistent, Bradman replied, that they would accept, but they still expected the Rivetts to dine with them at Frankston as well as per the original invitation.

Shirley Bradman was also on the move, but much farther afield. Shirley had got a job in Lincolnshire and would fly to England in January to take it up: 'Great excitement on her part – tremendous apprehension on mine'. Rivett's secretary was also departing. She had resigned and Bradman told his friend that he could not understand how she had lasted so long. He was sorry she was leaving, especially as it meant Bradman would now have to once again decode Rivett's handwritten notes. More drastically, the

Nancy (Nan) Rivett, an actress prior to her marriage to Rohan in 1947. Bradman adored her and the two couples were close friends.

Bradman as reporter, with England captain Len Hutton during the Ashes series in England, 1953.

Bradman and bodyline antagonist Douglas Jardine in the press box covering the 1953 Ashes series.

John, Jessie, Don and Shirley in the Bradman drawing room of their home in Kensington Park, Adelaide, 1956.

Jessie and Shirley watch Bradman drive at the 9th hole of the Kooyonga Golf Club during the club championship, June 1961. He made it to the quarter-finals that year.

Bradman (centre) with fellow Australian selectors Dudley Seddon (left) and Jack Ryder, assessing potential players for the 1964 Ashes tour of England.

The Australian Board of Control meeting at the South Australian Cricket Association's office, Adelaide, 1969 (Bradman seated second from right). Bradman was a progressive cricket administrator in the face of almost intractable institutional inertia.

Bradman tosses to decide play at the Prime Minister's cricket match, Manuka Oval, 1963. England captain Ted Dexter watches. Prime Minister Robert Menzies attended the match.

Bradman admired the public speaking ability of Rivett, pictured here mid-speech, and was a tough critic of his own: 'I hate making speeches & get infuriated when I feel I've made a bad one & people insist on telling me it was good.'

Rohan Rivett (seated) with Jessie Bradman (seated centre) and Nan Rivett (to her left) at Rhyll and David Rivett's twenty-first birthday party. Rhyll stands behind Jessie and Nan.

Bradman examines a biography of the 'black Bradman', George Headley, with West Indies captain Clive Lloyd, 1975. West Indies team manager Esmond Kentish stands behind Bradman. Bradman loved the West Indies' exciting style of play.

rollcall of deaths resumed. One recent evening Bradman had visited his great friend Eric Williams, a senior executive at the Bank of South Australia, 'and the next day bang'. On the positive side of the slate, Bradman believed he had forty more sheep but was not certain due to Mount Lofty fog. And the *Advertiser* had a new sports editor, Merv Agars: 'Great rejoicing at this on all sides.'

June 1967 saw an affectionate Bradman swipe at his friend's continuing animus to small town Adelaide's alleged big-timers. Bradman thanked Rivett for his letter which was welcome, he said, 'mainly because it showed a a humane side of your character which was quite foreign to me'. Rivett obviously believed that the attitude toward him of the OAFs – old Adelaide families – had contributed to his controversial departure from the *News*. 'You have only to finally give up your vendetta against the so-called establishment in this State (which from paragraph 3 still rankles) and I will now lift you from 99% to 100%.'

Rivett wanted Don and Jessie to travel overseas with him and Nan the following year, and Bradman told him his case for doing so was convincing. He couldn't say yes, however, since getting away for him would be so difficult: 'I can only say that if the chance does arise that we can make it, I will certainly let you know right away.' In the meantime he continued to provide detailed calls on potential portfolio changes, at Rivett's request. He was never too stretched to fit in a football comment. 'Bad luck for St. Kilda,' he signed off one letter towards the end of the 1967 football season.

Even exhaustion did not stop Bradman responding to Rivett's share queries. In August 1967 he wrote his second detailed letter in consecutive days about Rivett's portfolio. He had been flat to the boards, he told Rivett. 'I don't think I have hit the cot before midnight for over a fortnight,' he wrote. 'Even now I am up against time somewhat so please excuse brevity.'

The following month Rivett wrote urging Bradman to ease his workload. Bradman replied that he was just not in a position to do so. 'Yes the strictures contained in your letter were justified,' he said, 'but Rohan can I, at 59, resign from such things as the Board of Control, Selection Committee, Presidency SACA, & sundry boards which earn me a living? I would atrophy.' Short bursts of high activity were inevitable despite his determined efforts to strike a balance, Bradman said. Such spikes became more difficult when illness intervened, as occurred in September 1967 when Bradman wrote his reply.

The reciprocal looking out for each other continued when he returned to his theme of the previous month about Rivett's arrangements for the future. 'All I ask is that you get advice from a reliable and competent life man,' Bradman wrote, 'to assure that your present policies give you maximum protection.' There were powerful differences in the impact of various types of policies depending on their detail, he said. There were aspects that laymen could not understand, and expert advice was crucial. Bradman had got expert advice, even consulting an actuary as part of the process, and had been grateful for the result.

The old cricket network came in handy at strange times and for the oddest reasons. In October 1967 Rivett sought advice about a good nurseryman in the Bowral area where he considered buying a farm. Bradman replied that he had left Bowral forty years earlier and was out of touch. 'But if you are serious, write to my esteemed friend Alf Stephens, former mayor & captain [of the] Bowral cricket team. He would be delighted to advise a friend of mine.'

That same cricketing community was a source of occasional in-jokes with Rivett, too. In October 1967 Bradman teased Rivett about a just published article 're-rating' Melbourne's elite. How could Camberwell be omitted when the Rivetts lived there? He didn't wonder that Rivett had downgraded Toorak, however, since Bob Parish, an influential cricket administrator, had just bought a house there, swiped Bradman – mainly for his poodles, he thought.

While he never had too little time to lavish on correspondence with Rivett, Bradman was harried by other outside demands including ordinary ones faced by everyone, like bills. 'Every day the mail makes me exasperated because it consists about 90% of bills, requests to subscribe to charities, requests to speak at functions or contribute articles to publications & so on,' he grouched. Bradman dusted up Rivett over a previous letter in which he accused Rivett of 'thrashing me' about whether overs should consist of six or eight balls, the bowling rate per over, and the relative merits of various cricketers. But Bradman's three page riposte gave way in the end to a declaration that all that mattered was the Rivetts' impending visit in a fortnight's time.

Family worries were always uppermost in Bradman's mind. He responded to one set of Rivett's share queries despite tiredness. He had not had a decent sleep for some time, he said: 'Hope I'm coherent.' At the end of the extensive advice came the family sadness which he felt safe to share with Rivett. Their problems with John and Shirley had so dominated their existence, he wrote: 'I often wish we were free of family responsibility – as we should be by now – but alas it looks some distance off.'

The going got heavier as Christmas 1967 approached. The Bradmans had been looking forward to getting together with the

Rivetts, but Don wrote to Rohan on 13 December that the arrangements were off: Jessie had been taken seriously ill. They were together at a Rotary Club function at Hallett's Cove earlier that week when Jessie had been stricken with extraordinary pain and was rushed by ambulance to Royal Adelaide Hospital with a suspected coronary. It looked like she would not make it. It turned out to be a blood clot on the lung, a life-threatening condition, but luckily no underlying heart problem was evident. It would mean some time in hospital followed by a slow recovery period: 'she is a very sick girl'.

The Bradmans' Christmas plans were cancelled. Bradman had to deal with the forthcoming test and Shirley's imminent departure for England on 30 December as well as care for his much loved Jessie during her convalescence. 'The Bradmans were never ones to get minor troubles,' he told Rivett, '*but we shall return*'. He was not in the mood to discuss the state of the currency or the stockmarket or cricket and he knew Rivett would understand.

A few months later, things had steadied. Jessie was well 'within limits'; John was 'fair' and working hard, and things were peaceful at home without him. Shirley, 'splendid', was working happily as an assistant at a school in Cambridge; they had spoken by phone on her birthday. With the farm, on top of everything else, Bradman had been too busy for golf.

As Bradman approached his sixtieth birthday, Rivett triggered a candid character assessment from the great man, with his request for a television interview to mark the occasion. Bradman's long 'no' to the interview invitation revealed much about his own view of himself, of cricket and the media. The interview would be fine for the television station concerned, owned by Rupert Murdoch, and fine for the press, 'but what about poor old DB'? He thought the invitation was more about Murdoch wanting to use an interview with him as part of the pattern of cricket bashing that prevailed at the time.

'I am a small & insignificant figure in the world and even in the cricket world,' Bradman wrote in a fit of wishful thinking. Further, he declared himself an 'idealist' who believed the media had a duty to uplift and advance humanity rather than drag it down. The invitation in the current environment did not attract Bradman at all but he promised to discuss it with Rivett when he visited providing Rivett remained calm, listened and did not try to dominate him. 'Gosh you will laugh at all I've said,' Bradman wrote. 'I can imagine it. Old DB has gone off his rocker.'

Now, eight months after Jessie's near fatal medical emergency, she was watching Australia play England at Glamorgan. Bradman had told her, he recounted to Rivett, that the team seemed to be little inspired by her presence. Shirley, still working in England, had arranged accommodation with a coalminer who turned out, in fact, to have been a former bank manager. The other surprise was that he also turned out to be 'T.T.' – that is, teetotal. Shirley had told her father that three hours into a coffee party she really wanted a brandy, but her host had told her that only the rich drank. 'Like R.R.,' quipped Bradman.

Bradman and Rivett had been friends for more than a decade by 1968 and the pace of their exchanges had not slackened. On 31 August Bradman thanked Rivett for 'the meal, the telegram, the letters etc.' The quick letter traversed investment and cricket issues in some depth, crammed into a single-spaced typed page – no longer, Bradman explained, because he was in a hurry for dinner.

Some matters were sensitive but, given their investment relevance, Bradman did not hold back. For example, he sent Rivett a clipping from the *News* – the paper from which Rivett was sacked as editor by Murdoch – trumpeting a significant circulation increase: 'The News Racing Ahead', went the mock promotional one-sheet reproduced on the paper's front page. This could only have been cause for chagrin in Rivett.

In October 1968 Bradman told Rivett he was glad his friend was taking things a little easier. 'I'm trying to but gosh it is hard,' he went on. 'I get saddled with more and more voluntary stuff every day.' Rivett was mellowing, Bradman observed, commenting that he nevertheless still enjoyed his occasional 'flare-ups' like a recent reference to the Liberal premier of Victoria, Henry Bolte, as an 'amiable goat'. In a sunny mood, Bradman told a joke. 'Did you hear about the old man who turned 100,' he wrote. 'They asked him what it felt like. He said wonderful – I haven't got an enemy in the world. The buggers are all dead.'

The spring rains had made the farm, now carrying 34 sheep, a picture. But there were too many weeds and Bradman said that Jessie, who had been away, could come and lose a bit of weight helping him get rid of them. Shirley was fine, John all right but tending to tiredness – all in all the Bradmans were facing their problems and surmounting them, he said. There was some earnest discussion about the relative merits of the Sturt and Carlton football teams, and finally regards to the children and the ever-present salutation to Nan: 'My love to your beautiful wife.' Bradman had told Jessie about the evening he had spent with the Rivetts at their Port Willunga holiday house, which must have turned into a dry affair on the wine front. 'She said right – the next time we see those Rivetts,' he wrote to Rohan, 'we will take our own grog.'

The following month John appeared to be going downhill, 'desperately tired' and pessimistic about his exam results, and Bradman himself was back in the hands of his doctors for x-rays. Was Rohan, he queried hopefully, coming over for the test? Bradman said he couldn't pick the winner, though the golfing contest with Garfield Sobers was already settled. 'Anyway I gave Sobers a hiding at golf,' he wrote. 'He was humiliated by "the old man" as he put it.'

By early 1969 it was Shirley's health that dominated the family's concerns. She had spent seven weeks in hospital, Bradman told Rivett, and was only just about to return home. Yet Shirley was 'still bright and cheerful', he reported. As for himself Bradman said he was looking forward to the televised fight between world bantamweight boxing champion Lionel Rose and American fighter Alan Rudkin: 'Is it a set-up for Rose? Or is it Ansett's benefit? At least it's a great ad for this TV station.'

The following month Don and Jessie's firm booking for a golfing retreat at Frankston with friends Dr and Mrs Prest got in the way of an invitation to attend a party at the Rivetts' home in Melbourne. The golfing holiday was to last from 27 April to 7 May 1969 – a proper break, to be followed by a visit to the Bradman home by Jessie's sister, coming to see a degree conferred on her daughter. They would be with the Rivetts in spirit though, he assured their friends, and would drink a toast in their honour. 'Thank heaven my share advice will pay for the party Rohan,' Bradman quipped.

Again, a few months later, he had to knock back a Rivett

invitation. There was no chance of an imminent visit, Bradman wrote that August, since he was due in Sydney for a board meeting followed by a few trips over the summer. Bradman playfully contrasted his ongoing responsibilities with Rivett's more carefree Melbourne existence. 'What a lucky man you are to have a wife who can keep you in your old age with her skill,' Bradman wrote. 'And when that is allied to good looks, charm etc. well —?'

In fact, Rivett was finding the going hard writing *David Rivett*, an account of his father's life published three years later. Bradman pushed him on. The encouragement came more easily than usual since life at 2 Holden Street was humming along pretty smoothly. John was merely 'getting over-tired' rapidly, as usual for that time of year. 'We have our fingers crossed,' wrote Bradman.

He resisted Rivett's ideas about expansion on the rural front. The family's existing small holding was already almost beyond manageable size, given his other commitments, and Bradman said he looked forward to getting it to the point where it could tick over without close attention for six months at a time. Rivett, who himself was considering farming, wanted to know who was the pick of stock and station agents from Bradman's experience. Bennett's did their work, he advised, and did it most reliably. Bradman was amazed, he said, that Bennett's could be bothered with such a small client and treat them so well.

Bradman was buoyant in this winter of 1969, and a rare extravagance was one expression of it. 'You'll never believe me but I've traded the Valiant in on a Rover 2000,' he crowed to Rivett. 'What extravagance. I've always wanted one and in a moment of rashness I allowed myself to be talked into it.' Even the failure of the Rover's handbrake on day one, despite making him mad, couldn't spoil his pleasure, he liked it so much. 'That will probably be my last car,' he wrote.

The buoyancy did not last into spring. In October 1969 Bradman revealed despair 'in many directions'. Politics appalled him. The federal coalition government, including narrowly re-elected Prime Minister John Gorton, needed to 'get off their tails'. Labor victories at the state or federal level would lead to new taxes. Neither side of politics seemed capable of making the public sector efficient. Rohan's previous letter had made him shudder over the possibility of the touring Australian Test team getting caught by political violence in India. And on top of it all, Bradman's back pain had returned. The previous bout had lasted three months: 'If it lasts that long again I am going to be mighty bad tempered.'

On the plus side of the slate, John had finished lectures and was now swatting for his law exams. He and Jessie again had their fingers crossed. As always, Bradman sent '[our] love to your beautiful wife & the nips'.

Towards the end of 1969, Rivett consulted Bradman on the settling of some of his capital on his children. Better done while alive, heading off probate, Bradman responded, saying Rivett's plan looked sound to him: 'As you know I've done this for John & Shirley & they are now settled & can take care of themselves,' he wrote.

Bradman hoped Rivett was 'girding his loins for the Xmas feast'. At 2 Holden Street the mood was upbeat. John had finished his exams and was reasonably confident about the results – a positive sign. 'Gosh I hope he makes it,' Bradman wrote. 'He is 30. Time he got married, got [a] job & learnt the hard knocks.'

On Christmas Eve Bradman dashed off a note – 'the usual

imbecilic Xmas rush is on' – to arrange a mutually convenient date to get together in the New Year. There were two conditions: that Rivett not forget the red, and that 'Bray' was not invited. This was presumably poet and judge John Bray, known in Adelaide as 'Bray'.

Rivett had asked whether Bradman had read 'Haylen's book' – presumably former federal Labor MP Les Haylen's *Twenty Years' Hard Labor*, published in 1969. Bradman said he hadn't, but would on Rivett's recommendation 'even though I may be a George V man'. He had read Menzies' book though – presumably *Afternoon Light*, published in a Penguin edition in 1969 – which he judged 'poor'.

A bad back soon struck Bradman down again and it was not until the winter of 1970 that it improved to the point where he could resume playing golf. He wrote to Rivett at the end of June, apologising for a letter that was 'brief & scrappy because I am laid up in bed with a particularly nasty wog & feel rotten'. The dreadful flu had done the rounds of the family, first striking Shirley, now again living in Adelaide, then Jessie, who had gone to stay for a week with Shirley to nurse her, and then Don, who succumbed on a trip to Sydney.

Even laid low in bed back home, though, Bradman had the energy to fulminate about recent political events in England, South Australia's dire straits as an investment destination under Dunstan, and the problems of business making a dollar given 'irresponsible' union behaviour, especially in the manufacturing sector. Only the good news about his slowly recovering back and playfulness about Jessie at the end saved it from being a jeremiad. Lying sick in bed in the middle of winter, Bradman had to throw forward to the coming summer, half a year hence, before he could see any way of accepting Rivett's latest invitation for him and Jessie to visit.

But the next month, in August 1970, Rivett decided to visit, and he wanted to consult Bradman's stock and station agent for advice on beef cattle. Bradman pleaded for the visit dates which Rivett had failed to include in his letter about the trip. Bradman already had engagements on the evenings of 19, 20, 23, 25, 27, 28, 29 and 30 August and was due in Sydney on 31 August, 'hence you can understand my anxiety'. Bradman proposed that on the night of 26 August, the eve of his birthday, Rivett come to the Bradmans' home at 2 Holden Street. 'Love to your gorgeous wife,' he signed off.

Christmas 1970 saw some relief for Bradman over his perpetual worry about John's future. He reported to Rivett that John won credits in his year-end results for history, economics and law. 'That's the end,' he declared of John's long haul in equipping himself for the future.

Bradman accepted Rivett's invitation to a social gathering at his and Nan's home on 30 December but said that he could not stay the night. Pressing business the next morning compelled him to return to the Windsor Hotel that evening. He offered Jessie's and Shirley's apologies as they would not arrive in Melbourne in time for the occasion.

When it came to business dealings Bradman could be matter of fact to the point of brusqueness. At Rohan's request he had taken the manuscript of a book to the managing director of publisher Rigby, of which Bradman was a director. The managing director had read it personally and, reluctantly, decided it was not for Rigby 'so the matter is closed'.

Pressure of business may have contributed to Bradman's brevity. September 1971 saw Bradman knock back another social invitation for him and Jessie from Rohan and Nan. He hoped the Rivetts would enjoy themselves but things would be tough for the Bradmans for the next four months, he wrote: 'after that I can see some daylight'. Managing the diplomacy surrounding the World XI venture was one major challenge, fulfilling longstanding commitments was another. Don and Jessie had to go to New Zealand in November, he told Rivett, to fulfil an obligation made eight years earlier to speak at a crippled children's fundraiser for the Murray Halberg Trust. 'Dear old Dot Grundy', a close friend of Jessie's, died that week he added to the bottom of the quick note.

By then sixty-two years old, Bradman's commitments seemed to intensify, not diminish. In the winter of 1971 he was exhausted, but still pushing on with a punishing schedule. 'Am desperately tired,' he confided. 'Have had one night home in the last 9 and Jessie celebrated by inviting (unannounced) some unwelcome guests.'

Bradman had been so desperately busy that he had not been able to attend to the minutes of a recent board meeting in Sydney, and was now 'up to my ears' in talks about the disputed future of Adelaide Oval. He asked that his thanks be passed on to Nan and Rhyll for recent letters to him, and he wished Rohan luck for the imminent Walkley Awards. The only award Bradman had won of late, he wrote, was that of 'Pekinese Pup' which one hostile correspondent had conferred. Still, he said, he nixed the slur by replying he would rather be a Pekinese pup than a yellow dog, bitch, mongrel or cur.

Autumn 1972 brought the nadir in the family drama centred on John's difficulties being a Bradman. In a bid to differentiate himself from his crushingly famous father, John changed his surname by deed poll to 'Bradsen'. On 13 March a broken-hearted Don wrote to Rivett and described events as they had unfolded. The *Advertiser* told John they were running the story come what may, virtually forcing him into explaining his action lest the journalist concerned infer some other reason. It was front page news in both the *Advertiser* and, in what Don described as the cruellest story he had ever read, in the *News*. 'If ever a story was calculated to crucify and ridicule a decent person, this was it and it is something for which I shall never forgive them,' he wrote of the *News* story.

John's decision revealed deep ambivalence about his famous name. He wanted to be different – not 'Bradman', but, instead, 'Bradsen' – yet the change was not a decisive one. There was a congruity about the names that, arguably, gave little differentiation at high cost to family feelings and with much public controversy. 'You can well imagine how Jessie and I feel,' Don wrote.

But after talking with John they told him they understood his feelings and were prepared to wear the hurt to themselves 'and all it means'. Would it really help John though, he queried, and if not wouldn't it leave him worse off than before? The whole process had reinforced the issue John had, in fact, tried to resolve, with headlines like 'Bradman's son changes his name' appearing rather than 'John Bradman changes his name', Don pointed out. At the same time his own scepticism about whether it was really such a burden to John crept out in an ironic reference to 'this desperate thing with which John has found himself unable to live'.

Don begged off commenting on other interesting aspects of Rivett's previous letter as 'I feel so flat I haven't the heart'. It had not been a cheerful letter, he acknowledged, 'but I know you'll understand'. He asked Rohan to write again.

Rivett did. It was a period when the friendship, and the chance to unburden oneself through the correspondence, was at its most precious. Bradman's reply was even more troubled than his earlier letter. Shirley was hospitalised at the end of March with dire headaches, getting worse and leading to blackouts. Tests were conducted to rule out a tumour – invasive tests, carried out while conscious, and leading to truly terrible headaches as the brain slowly recovered from them. She was now at home with the Bradmans at 2 Holden Street but had missed 'her beloved fete at Ashford on Saturday at which Jessie, in charge of the flower stall, raised nearly $600 for the littlies'.

Bradman's layman's guess was that the problem was associated with Shirley's disability, but the doctors assured him it was not. They were unable to identify the root of the problem, however, and the long term outlook was not positive, Bradman told Rivett.

John had only seen him once since the 'fateful day' the name change became public, and the matter of his name change did not come up. How could he fail to develop a guilty conscience over the move, Bradman queried, even though it was understood within the family that the name change was not driven by bad feelings towards Don and Jessie? John's mind had become dominated by a feeling that he lacked individuality but questions lingered: 'I feel it is more than what appears on the surface.'

Yet Bradman did not look for deeper reasons inside John. Instead he blamed the political climate of the period, when the forces of the 1960s counterculture were still working their way through the system. John's beard told the story, he confided to Rivett. It was about youth's rejection of the older generation and its values – 'the system, the establishment or something'. John had become a revolutionary at heart, he believed. Bradman despaired that John's fine intellect, capable of achieving great things, had become riven with questions of individuality.

John had been assured by Don that becoming 'Bradsen' would make no difference to their relationship, but to Rohan he confided he could not really ever quite think the same of John again: 'Even though I understand, the rejection of my name and all the hopes and ambitions that any father would normally have for a son, are a deep wound which I will have to bear silently to the end.' Bradman apologised for the letter being so personal but told Rivett he believed his friend would understand.

And he did. Rivett quickly replied with reassurance and relayed both his and Nan's take on John's actions. Bradman subsequently agreed with Nan's analysis that John 'wants it both ways'. Therein lay one of the difficulties, Bradman revealed, since Jessie was passionately committed to easing John through the problem with sympathy. Don, conversely, thought he needed what would now be called tough love. In his view, John ought to have had the guts to face up to the world and get on with it. It was the only time in the correspondence that a difference of opinion in the marriage – other than the occasional minor disagreement flowing from Jessie's gregariousness – was disclosed. Wrote Bradman: 'I shall carry this cross to my grave . . .' He hoped the matter would recede to the background as the years went by. 'But I shall always be grateful,' he told Rivett, 'for your understanding of a personal tragedy which if not unique, is very close to being so.'

The fracture between Bradman and John worsened in the ensuing weeks. By mid-winter the remaining veil Bradman had over his feelings about John's behaviour was torn away in his correspondence with Rivett. Rivett had made some comments and suggestions about John in a recent letter, for which Bradman thanked him but signalled that from then on it was up to John to make his own way. He had done so much for John, 'physically, mentally and financially', without any hint, he said, of gratitude in return. There was 'nothing but cynical criticism of everything I do or say and an apparent hatred of the legacy I have given him in my name and a detestation for all the things I believe in and stand for'.

The tragedy was that no young man in Adelaide had such tremendous advantage or public sympathy as John, Bradman wrote, and it had been thrown away because he could not accept life as it was rather than how he wanted it to be. Bradman predicted John would come to regret the name change, and even reverse it, but forecast that it might not happen until Bradman was dead 'when I think the full magnitude of the heart break he has caused will dawn upon him'.

It was clear that, while the immediate incident had been dealt with in a dignified and conciliatory manner at the time of the media storm in March, relations between Bradman and John in the following few months had become steeped in deep mutual resentment and barely submerged anger. Bradman had not liked John changing his name but had gone along with it in support of John's hope that it would transform his situation. But since it had happened, Bradman's support in the face of John's private behaviour had become an intolerable contradiction. Bradman could not accept that John was willing to draw on his resources and favours – to enjoy the benefits of being his son – at the same time as he treated Bradman 'like an outcast'. It was a question of mental maturity, he argued, and Jessie's sympathy for John merely delayed his development. Bradman, in contrast, wanted to kick John in the pants and 'force him to take the independence he claims to crave'. It had created a shocking situation at home, he wrote, but it was a domestic problem with which they alone had to grapple.

At least the news was better about Shirley. Her health had improved to the point that she was able to resume light work at Ashford House School, though with two afternoons off a week on her specialist's advice: 'She remains sweet and brave despite her burdens . . .' Shirley would be fine with him and Jessie as a backstop during difficult times, Bradman said, and financially they had secured her position for life, but they worried about how she would fare, other than in a material sense, when they were both gone.

Again Bradman had poured out his heart to Rivett. The letter had been written quickly – partly because Rivett was shortly to travel overseas with daughter Rhyll, making time of the essence to meet postal deadlines. But Bradman added a quick rider. Rohan should consider looking up Bradman's best friend in London for lunch – Esso executive David Drummond, a cricket fanatic and a 'real whizzer' at his job. Drummond may even know of some job prospects for Rhyll, who was to accompany her father to Britain. Bradman said he would alert Drummond to the possibility of a call: 'You would enjoy the contact if nothing else.'

Bradman's gloom of the winter of 1972 gave way to some better times the following year. At the end of summer the Bradmans dined with the Rivetts for the first time in too long, with the result that Don and Jessie talked more than their usual share and the evening passed quickly: 'The wine was good and the food was good and at least temporarily one was able to forget the woes of this world, for which we were grateful.' Nan and Rohan looked better than he and Jessie had ever seen them, he wrote.

But it was swings and roundabouts on the home front. Rivett's previous letter had contained good news on the achievements and situation of the Rivett children. He replied that Rohan and Nan could bask in the reflected glory. When it came to 'what's been happening with the Brads', as Don put it, things were more mixed.

Bradman reported that John was at last finding his legs, careerwise, in the law. John had decided over the summer to do his articles in order to keep the option open of becoming a practising lawyer, and had started at Finlayson & Co in February. One month there had reversed John's previous view of articled clerkship as a legal relic that should be abolished, Bradman wrote. John enjoyed the work and was learning a lot. At the same time he was teaching part-time at the University of Adelaide law school, playing in a jazz band and 'works like a navvy' on the farm. 'Regrettably his attitude towards me changes little though I believe in his heart he is gradually seeing the light,' Bradman wrote. 'Pride won't yet let him admit it.'

Things had taken a downturn for Shirley, however, with increasing strain on Jessie, who was far from well. The work at Ashford House School had become too much for Shirley and she had resigned. At a loose end, she had begun spending most of her time at the Bradmans' Holden Street home. Shirley's situation, for which there seemed to be no prospect of long term improvement, only further gradual decline, 'is rather eating Jessie's heart out'.

Jessie's blood condition continued to bother her; she lived on a knife edge when it came to her health, Bradman told Rivett. Jessie suffered some bleeding around the lungs, and was especially vulnerable during hot weather. As things were she just had to get some rest and Bradman had agreed reluctantly to Jessie travelling with her two sisters to England in May for a few months' break. 'Thank goodness my own health seems to be standing up well,' Bradman wrote. 'Lessening the cricket load has made things a bit easier.'

His comment came amidst a rollcall of illness and death. Bradman recounted how he had sat next to Victorian cricket administrator Bill Dowling the previous Wednesday night in Melbourne, at the inaugural Victorian Cricket Association dinner for the year where he was to present the Jack Ryder Medal. Dowling collapsed without warning in the middle of his speech, downed by a heart attack in front of the assembled guests. The Friday before that Bradman's best friend in New Zealand, New Zealand cricket association chief Gordon Leggat, died of a heart attack aged forty-six. That weekend former South Australian Stock Exchange president John Manning collapsed and died. Despite feeling besieged by disaster, Bradman still sent love to Nan from him and Jessie, and said how glad he was that her painting was going well.

Bradman, now sixty-four years old, was still going at almost full tilt. When Rivett wrote in autumn 1973 that he and Nan would visit Adelaide the following week and wanted to get together, it was a case of finding a crack in the diary into which the treasured friends could be squeezed. On the Monday, Bradman replied, he had board meetings for Clarkson's, City Mutual and SACA, all of which he chaired. Tuesday night was Rotary. Wednesday he would be guest speaker at the South Australian Umpires Association dinner where he was to present the Cricketer of the Year trophy. Thursday he had an F.H. Faulding board meeting all day 'but the evening is free so that is the night it will have to be', at the Rivetts' choice of venue.

The first signs of Bradman thinking about easing up came that winter. In July he told Rivett he had announced his retirement as SACA president, effective from September. The letter was sent in time to meet Rohan and Nan on their return from overseas. 'You lucky people,' he steamed jocularly, pointing out he was stuck at home while not only the Rivetts were travelling the world but Jessie was touring Norway and England and 'other lovely places'. Still, he rationalised, someone had to stay and make sure Shirley was all right, and it was his turn. John, he noted briefly, had married.

By spring Bradman had cleared a few decks, animated by the idea that it was 'utterly ridiculous that time never seems to permit us to sit down & chat at leisure'. He was now retired as an Australian cricket selector, a state selector, ACB chairman, SACA president and Clarkson's director. 'Am almost unemployed,' he joked to Rivett.

What's more Bradman was cheered by 'very good news' on Shirley's health and Jessie's return from Europe. Jessie was refreshed by the trip and once more able to give Shirley – recently returned home from another hospital stay – the attention she needed. After a fortnight at the Bradmans' home Shirley would be well enough to move back into her own flat, he told Rivett. In the New Year he hoped she would be well enough to find further employment.

But a month later, in October, Bradman's still heavy commitments were obvious as Rivett sought to arrange a get-together between the two couples in December. Bradman asked for latitude as he already had four dinners scheduled in the week concerned, eight weeks out from the Rivetts' visit.

In April 1974, on his return from an overseas trip with Nan, Rivett reminded Bradman of their last meal together with Nan and Jessie at the McLaren Vale restaurant 'The Barn', in the heart of the Fleurieu Peninsula's prime winemaking region. Bradman recalled with pleasure the evening they spent together, as well as a bet made that night which Don had won: 'But I did warn you in advance that you would lose the bet and I only went on because of your insistence.'

Don and Jessie would themselves be off soon – to England for two months for a charitable engagement and to visit friends, probably for the last time. Bradman's second best friend in England had visited him and Jessie at Christmas time, and they had planned to stay with him for a few days on the forthcoming trip. In 'blooming health' at Christmas, the friend was buried mid-April. Bradman was not being gloomy, just 'factual', he told Rivett: 'One has to face up to the realities of life when confronted with them.'

This direct squaring up to reality was typical of Bradman. It was evident in the same letter, too, when he addressed Rivett's account of troubles he had experienced with the publisher Rigby, of which Bradman remained a director. Bradman said he was distressed that Rivett had suffered the experience recounted, and that there had been a change in the managing directorship of Rigby in the intervening period. Bradman said he would personally bring it to the new managing director's attention. In a sensitive but explicit statement of the delicacies concerned, Bradman reminded Rivett that management issues were not usually the domain of a company's board but that, 'for the sake of our friendship apart altogether from the merits of the matter', he would take it forward, to the top. He felt obliged, he said, that it be investigated properly: 'I do not expect that you feel I have any responsibility to go further.'

Hard realities were, in fact, closing in quickly on Bradman. The otherwise enjoyable trip to England the previous year had been marred by health problems which led him to give up public speaking. He had addressed just two dinners in the preceding twelve months, to fulfil commitments made before the trip. Hundreds of invitations had been declined, and he gave the same response to an invitation from Rivett to address the Press Club: 'I feel rather bad about turning you down but after some 40 years of doing this sort of thing I must take a break and hope you'll understand.'

It was part of a rationalisation of activity rather than an absolute retreat. Bradman's company directorships remained demanding, 'and with the economy as it is that becomes rather a nightmare'. Jessie's continuing poor health was a worry. Relations with John remained brittle. John's appointment as a full-time member of the University of Adelaide law school staff had at least enabled Bradman to 'divorce myself from his affairs because he can handle his own'. (John became a successful legal academic with a solid publishing record, and remained at the University of Adelaide for most of his career.) He reported to Rivett that John was a candidate for councillor in the Adelaide Hills township of Crafers without further comment. 'Thank goodness Shirley is going through a good patch and I am okay,' he wrote. 'Can't afford to be anything else.'

Rohan had related one of his own problems in his previous letter: troubles concerning the Rivetts' long-owned cottage at Port Willunga. Bradman sympathised but advised his friend to fix the problem quickly in case 'Donnie' (Dunstan) declared Willunga a nudist beach as he had Maslins Beach, a little further north. Squatters would not be far behind, he predicted.

The Rivetts were about to travel overseas and Bradman wished them well, adding that he himself could not bear going to the Middle East just then though he understood that the Rivetts' deep engagement with international affairs would make it worthwhile. Instability in the Middle East intensified at that time. Economic peril was about at home. The juxtaposition led Bradman into musing about optimism and pessimism. He cited businessman Moxon Simpson's quip that optimists do crossword puzzles in ink while pessimists wear braces *and* belts. Bradman said his own pessimism was the kind which made him insure against fire not because he believed his home would burn down but because 'I cannot afford to take the risk'.

One brief line – just eleven words – in this four page letter of single-spaced typing provoked a quietly passionate, closely argued response from Rivett. It was Bradman's comment, buried in parentheses among his desperate railings about the economic mismanagement of Australia at the time, that 'your public utterances seem to run counter to your private behaviour'.

Rivett's response – three typed pages, single-spaced – was dated four days later, and was written two hours before his and Nan's departure for Indonesia, the first port of call on an extensive tour of Asia and the Middle East. While sent on the verge of departure, the care with which it was drafted suggests a deliberately measured response by Rohan at odds with his known tendency to tempest.

Rivett opened by honouring the friendship between the two couples, noting especially that Nan 'rates it as a very precious possession'. He accepted Bradman's knockback of his invitation to address the Press Club. The invitation remained open for a later time when there was perhaps something Bradman felt so strongly about that the forum could be useful to him. With the politesse out of the way, Rivett addressed the nub: 'I'm sure there is nothing inconsistent between my public utterances and my private behaviour.' The burden of Bradman's fleeting sledge, as Rivett perceived it, was that Rivett was a rich man who generally took the socialist side of the argument. He rejected it, at length and comprehensively.

'There is nothing inconsistent in espousing these causes and seeking to earn as much money as possible for Nan and the children,' Rivett wrote. 'Today the three of them can well provide for themselves and all my financial responsibilities rest on younger and better shoulders. Therefore I can devote my money to things I believe in, e.g. the David Rivett [Asian] Memorial Library at Queens [College, University of Melbourne], the Freemasons, good causes at places at which I remain indebted for my education, and so on. Other people with my income buy yachts or swimming pools or mistresses or something which pleases them. I prefer to use it to try and bring enlightenment to our community, particularly such suicidal tendencies as the Menzies policies towards Asia.'

Rivett declared he had spent the last nine years of the Liberal Party's twenty-three year long federal reign 'trying to expose the futility of trying to win wars in Asia by the methods of the Americans (with us as little-sir-echoes) employed in Indo-China'. After all that time, with federal government policies tilted towards the 'haves', Rivett argued, it was fair enough for policies to be tilted for three or perhaps even five years towards the 'have-nots'.

Just because one might be sympathetic to the public ownership of some assets and enterprises did not mean that membership of the Athenaeum, the Beefsteaks or the Fitzroy Football Club was out of bounds, Rivett continued. 'I happen to enjoy all three,' he wrote. 'I need the contacts and information obtained by entertaining in these circles for my work and I don't regard it as money spent on frivolous self-indulgence.'

Rivett told Bradman he was wrong to be appalled at Australia's medium and long term economic prospects – the nation was too well endowed with resources in general, and in brainpower in both the public and private sectors in particular, for prospects not to be bright. He conceded the Whitlam Government's economic policies had been 'erroneous and costly' but argued that the seeds of the disastrous inflation Australia experienced were sown by the Liberal McMahon Government before Whitlam came to power. 'I can't think of a better man than Bill Hayden to put us back on the right course,' he wrote of the then newly appointed treasurer.

Conceding there might well have to be a showdown with the unions, Rivett nevertheless tried to assuage the unemployment fears Bradman regularly expressed both in response to maintaining jobs for the workers of companies of which he was a director, and more generally. There was no shortage of jobs for those who really wanted them, Rivett claimed, before seguing to international perceptions of Australia under Whitlam – a topic which Bradman did not much address.

'At any rate we can now hold our heads up in Asia and meet every challenge eye to eye,' Rivett wrote. 'The chances of the children of John [Bradman] or David or Keith [Rivett] having to fight for their existence as we did in 1942 are now perhaps five to one against. From 1949 to 1972 when we pulled out of Vietnam those chances probably went from evens to five to one on simply because we seemed to every intelligent Asian racist, self-centred and to be represented by the snobbish arrogance of a Prime Minister who only reluctantly ever acknowledged that Asians existed.'

The internationalism of Rohan and Nan emerged strongly, in contrast. Nan had developed an interest in 'the petro-dollar men' and they were off to get a first hand view of the Middle East, visiting Iran, Lebanon and Syria. 'This is my favourite ground,' he wrote, 'as it may be yours! But my reason is that it is one of the most knowledgeable crowds I have found anywhere between Barbados and Bombay or Birmingham.'

Bradman may or may not have been winding Rivett up, deliberately provoking his affluent establishment friend. If that was his intention, it worked – perhaps too well. Rivett responded comprehensively to a small but pointed barb which one senses had probably been levelled often before by others to Rivett's great annoyance. The divide rested on the heavier weighting Bradman gave to domestic economic and employment issues over international relations compared to Rivett, who weighted them in the opposite direction.

In his letter Rivett rebutted many points which Bradman had not, in fact, made in the letter which so provoked him. Bradman's views on Vietnam, for example, and the conduct of Australian and US policy towards South-East Asia, or Asia generally, do not merge in the correspondence. Bradman was so desperately worried about Australia's domestic economic plight, and especially the consequences for employment, that one senses he did not have room to worry about much else.

Rivett closed solicitously but without the usual salutations of love. 'Please give our affectionate good wishes to Jessie, Shirley and John,' he wrote, 'and do look after yourself until we can indeed crack that bottle together.'

The slight frost which tinged the relationship in the Whitlam Government's final winter, on Rivett's side at least, did not last. By summer Bradman was welcoming the travellers back home and pinning down dates for the two couples to meet in January of 1976. Rohan had asked Don to review a list of shares for him, and the political discourse resumed on very friendly terms.

The correspondence slowed down at times that year. Bradman blamed the fates. He could barely recall a time of such demands and being 'less fitted to cope'. Several close friends had died, others were divorcing despite his and Jessie's best efforts to help, business demands were complex and his health was fragile – no doubt exacerbated by stress, he admitted.

'In the midst of this I had to make three interstate trips including that terrible three week Sydney–Brisbane journey including "BACK TO BOWRAL" which was fun for everyone else but a nightmare for me,' he wrote. 'Literally hundreds of friends and relatives with the demanding query "don't you remember me?", mostly people now aged 65 to 85 whom I had not met for nearly 50 years.'

Were Rohan and Nan off to Manila, he wanted to know; had Rhyll, then working for CRA, left for the US yet? For their part Jessie was well, Shirley happy and John 'becoming more human', giving Bradman glimmers of hope. 'The only Bradman crock is the old man,' he said. 'Still I'm lucky to have gone so far so well seeing that I've played or administered cricket for just half the whole history of test matches.'

Whatever the travails, Bradman barely slowed down. He dashed off a letter 'in a tearing hurry because I have to see my bank manager and I want to get the pleasant bit over first'. Bradman passed on the address in Oslo of John's former fiancée, in case the Rivetts visited Scandinavia on their forthcoming European trip. Then there were the arrangements for linking up when he and Jessie were in Melbourne for the Centenary Test celebrations. And there was approval for the Rivetts' decision to sell, after such a long time, the Port Willunga house where so many good family holidays had been enjoyed, and which had been the site of several convivial dinners with Don and Jessie. 'Sincere apologies for the typing,' he begged off. 'You are about the only person I would send this to, because yours is worse.'

It was in March 1977 that Rivett flagged to Bradman a surprise dinner for Nan at their Camberwell home scheduled for 17 October. Key friends were getting even older, and frailer, making the old connections even more precious and important to enjoy and honour. Ray Robinson was a case in point.

'Ray Robbie was with us for four hours,' Rivett wrote in his March letter. 'He is frightfully frail and does not always latch on to the subject of conversation. But I think this is partly deafness. I am praying he hangs on long enough to make that cricket writers' dinner at a Bloomsbury Hotel in April.' Before the year was out the mortality of the Bradmans and Rivetts themselves would be brought home, but that early autumn the encroaching twilight for some was not yet perceptible. In the meantime, Rivett was focused on the trip he and Nan were shortly to take to Baghdad, Norway and England. 'Trust you can keep October 17 for the dinner I mentioned to Jessie,' he reminded Don.

Within weeks, Jessie suffered a major heart attack. Bradman wrote to Rivett on Anzac Day 1977 to tell him, realising their friends were probably unaware of it. He hastened to get the message through before the Rivetts left for Europe. Jessie, he told Rivett, was still bedridden and very ill. Bradman confided how upset he was, yet not surprised since Jessie had received many warnings about the hectic pace at which she lived but would not slow down: 'On the humourous side I tell her she has let Dunstan off the hook because he can't make me Guv'nor with a sick wife.'

On their return Nan wrote asking about Jessie's condition and prospects. The doctors were loath to operate, Bradman replied, because the risks outweighed the likely reward. There had been some improvement, but it was slow. Jessie could just manage to walk around the block. On the positive side of the slate, though, her general health was good and 'her spirit is magnificent'. It appeared that her condition had stabilised to the point where a useful if sedentary life was still possible. In the midst of all this, Bradman had himself been operated on for a growth in the bowel, luckily benign: 'I'm still not all that hot & altogether life has been quite a burden.'

The psychological adjustment for Jessie was enormous. Bradman reported further on her slow progress – that she was able to do a little more: 'But to see such a vital person confined to such a low level of activity is terribly sad.'

By September things had turned sharply for the worse. Despite the risks, the doctors advised there was little future for Jessie without triple bypass surgery. While the Rivetts were celebrating on 17 October, the Bradmans would be praying, and unable to be in Camberwell with their great friends. 'I am desperately concerned but she is brave & has a great will to live,' Bradman relayed, along with Jessie's love to them both. On top of it all John had suffered a mild heart attack three weeks earlier. The dark clouds were banking up all at once.

Rivett replied immediately, urging Bradman to let him track down leading heart surgeon Allan Hobbs with whom Rivett had served hard time in a Japanese prisoner of war camp during World War II: 'In the 35 years since I met him in prison camp I have never known him to let anyone down.' Rivett was stunned, too, by the news of John who, he observed, had always looked so fit. 'I suppose,' Rivett wrote, 'the gods decided that the price of making you famous through at least three quarters of your own lifetime – an extraordinarily rare human condition – is the appalling catalogue of ills befalling Jessie, John and Shirley.'

Against this backdrop Don and Jessie were shattered by an early morning phone call from Nan telling them that Rohan had suddenly died. Don wrote to Nan immediately saying that he and Jessie were desperate with grief and at her disposal if there was anything at all that she needed. Sadly the funeral was something they would miss as Jessie's heart surgery, which they had to risk despite the uncertainty about her likely survival, was imminent.

'As we cannot undo God's will, let us be thankful for Rohan's great life,' Don wrote. 'You & he had wonderful times together, you are blessed with fine loving children & in time will overcome your sorrow & fulfil your own very worthwhile life.'

7 *The Private Don*

'. . . my friends are far more numerous among the rank and file than the upper crust. All in all I wouldn't have it any other way.'

— Don Bradman

If Australians declared mortals gods the way the old Romans did, Don Bradman would be first in the pantheon. He was short (170 centimetres), he was slight (65 kilograms), he was modest, he was self-contained – and rather than being one of the boys he was his own person and hang the consequences. Bradman was highly intelligent and steadfast, qualities which people sensed as well as saw expressed on the field. There was a compelling dimension of mystery about him flowing, perhaps, from his combination of quietude and spectacular sporting virtuosity. Virtually from the moment his test cricket career began in 1928, Australians attached themselves to this ordinary-looking but brilliant man in a way that felt for them somehow life redeeming, his goodness and greatness seeming to touch and renew.

Cricket historian David Frith correctly locates Bradman's lasting fame in his ability to make runs in abundance, almost twice as many on average as the next greatest batsmen of the game from any other time or place. But Frith also identified how deeply Bradman was absorbed into the fibre of Australia's national being, its core open, wounded and vulnerable from the Great Depression during which Bradman's star shone brightest.

> He meant so much to Australians, even to those for whom cricket was a remote phenomenon. He drew them closer to it. He inhabited their minds and souls. In these terrible times he represented hope and defiance and indestructibility. People could turn their backs on the dreadfulness of the moment and find some sort of succour in the triumphs of The Don. It came close to religious devotion and dependence. Woe to the man or force that sought to harm him.

What a burden for any mortal. John Bradman was wise to caution after his father's death in 2001 against deification. He knew his father was human; he saw and experienced the pressures such strong sentiment created during his father's lifetime. In any case, Australia is secular in state and spirit. As our culture in so many ways shows every day, Australians are more inclined to glorify the person who can hit a ton rather than one who can hit the devil for six.

The greater the distance from his active cricket career, the more revered Bradman became among a public jaded with the sledging-, sex-, and betting-scandalised sport once synonymous with standards and civilisation. Death in 2001 did trigger The Don's final ascension to a place in the Australian psyche occupied by none before or since. Like old-fashioned royalty, his ability to remain above the fray was underpinned by an equally old-fashioned technique: silence. His legend expanded as the decades ticked over. The odd shabby tale pushed around here or there failed to stick; memories of his magnificent sporting career and its preternatural statistics were not spoiled.

Bradman drew a sharp demarcation after his playing days ended in 1949, at forty-one years old, between private and public life. Even his considerable ongoing involvement as a cricket administrator and selector was conducted with lips firmly sealed. But in those five post-playing decades, Bradman lived an intensely active life, not only as a cricket administrator but as a stockbroker, small farmer, husband, father and, to a modest and declining number of people, friend.

Rivett was one such friend – an especially close one. The letters chronicling the friendship between Bradman and Rivett show that relationships between Australian men don't have to be flattened into the cattle crush of 'mateship', the overwhelmingly dominant model on offer. Taciturn conversation, emotion restrained to the point of code, and the foreswearing of confidences that could embarrass the discloser and enhance the recipient's relative power are key mateship conventions.

In contrast, Bradman's relations with Rivett were warm, confiding, and full of trust embodied in voluminous, detailed exchanges. As he relayed candid views on cricket, politics and business along with his pleasures and problems at home on handwritten and, often, closely typed page after page to Rivett, he was inscrutable to the wider world. Intelligence, passion and wry humour were strictly contained by Bradman in his circumspect public life. But with Rivett, the real Bradman – the whole of Bradman – could safely wrestle over the big issues of the day, and of their lives.

The letters reveal Bradman's underlying positions clearly. On cricket it was that the game should be bright, entertaining and, while played fairly and to high standards of personal behaviour, played to win. On investment, Bradman looked for strong net assets and positive earnings trends, with a bias for capital growth over high yields. As a director, especially during the economic challenges of the 1970s, he placed a high premium on maintaining jobs, was frustrated by government regulatory caprice and indifference to inflation, and was preoccupied with questions of productivity. On journalism, he believed too many reporters ignorant of cricket were covering the great game, bent on negative reporting. And on family, it was love, loyalty and a steady slog through travails looking for sunshine on the other side. Bradman wrote like a dream, and he had a consistency of outlook, temperament and purpose that would have suited him perfectly for politics had he not been so appalled by it.

There is no whiff of the anti-Catholicism which has been an undercurrent of criticism promoted by his knockers. If it existed it would surely have emerged in this voluminous correspondence, especially since Rivett was a Mason. There is also an explicit commitment to the health and growth of cricket free of nationalistic arrogance or racist taint. For 'the good of the game' was the standard by which he judged things. Developing cricket abroad was a recurring theme, as was respect for the sensitivities of the countries concerned.

Nor was Bradman politically partisan, despite the best efforts of conservative politicians from Menzies to Howard to appropriate him by association. Quite the reverse, the letters show that Bradman was policy-driven and deeply sceptical that either side of politics was up to the task of doing what was needed to govern Australia well. He was explicitly and consistently non-party political, a position he underlined to Rivett on more than one occasion. The policies he wanted implemented bear remarkable similarity to the low-inflationary growth, productivity-oriented economic agenda of the Hawke and Keating governments (1983–96). In espousing such a policy agenda from the 1960s onwards, Bradman showed remarkable prescience.

The value of Bradman and Rivett's friendship appears beyond price from the letters. Best friends does not begin to describe it. Mateship is not the term Bradman would have used even though the relationship embodied the concept's ideal: loyalty, fidelity and mutual reliance in tough times. It is conspicuous that the term 'mate' is used on less than a handful of occasions in the more than one hundred letter correspondence, and on two of those occasions used with acid sarcasm during one of his rare fights with Rivett.

Ray Robinson, Bradman's favourite Australian cricket writer, provides a clue to this attitude. He recounts hazing of the young Bradman by his cricket elders during early tours – 'japemanship to a heartless extreme unlikely to be forgotten'. Bradman's talent set him so far apart from his team-mates, on and off the field, that it was virtually guaranteed to isolate him from them even had there been goodwill all round. His preference for a cup of tea and some classical music after a day's play instead of a night carousing round the bar made him most definitely not one of the boys – and the boys didn't like it. In fact Bradman's earliest social experience within Australian test cricket teams is a reminder of the flipside of the mateship phenomenon: exclusion. There are 'mates' and there are 'others'. If you are an 'other', you are made to pay a price; and the 'other' can be other men as well as the groups already recognised as being excluded by mateship culture. The contrast between his difficulty early in his Test career being accepted within the small groups that are cricket teams and the way he was taken to the bosom of the nation as a whole is fascinating.

Bradman appears never to have been a 'mate' within the Australian cricket scene. He had friends, not mates, and the distinction is significant. Bradman double steel reinforced his inner hardiness and got on with cricket and life his way, content in his own company and judgement, letting the rest continue as they pleased. The contrast between his approach to bodyline and that of much of the rest of the team is a case in point.

Even a Bradman sceptic could hardly fail to spend time with the letters without concluding that, while he was definitely a man of his times and milieu in the obvious senses, he was nevertheless a good and steadfast one. Spending most of one's life in Adelaide was necessarily limiting in certain respects. Not fully appreciating television's impact on elite sport and the potential earning power of sportspeople that would result being chief among them; the advent of World Series Cricket did not enter his imaginings until well too late. It made the demands of modern players for better pay and conditions incomprehensible to him: they seemed so much better off already compared to the remuneration of the Depression era cricketers of his prime. It was a blind spot in half a lifetime's cricket administration that was otherwise directed toward progressive change.

If Australians are to have a secular god, there could be worse choices than one who was upright, loyal, sceptical, loved his wife, stuck by his at times troubled son, delighted in his daughter despite her special difficulties and looked out for his friends – as well as being a sporting legend who put the good of the game before jingoistic interests. In a world hungry for heroes, disappointment is so often the upshot. But the Bradman letters in the National Library's Rivett Papers will burnish Bradman's place in the Australian pantheon. Few intimate correspondences would yield such an unequivocal result.

Endnotes

Each endnote marks the beginning of the section to which the citation relates.

Manuscript (MS) references are to the Bradman letters in the Rivett Papers, MS 8049, National Library of Australia, Canberra.

CHAPTER 1

'I think most . . . others say so.' MS 8049/2/B120, 7/8/68

'In my few . . . faithfully served mankind.' MS 8049/2/B147, 24/9/71

The Bradman letters . . . afternoon daily newspaper. 5/5/53, MS 8049/2/Bradman 1, Papers of Rohan Rivett, MS 8049, National Library of Australia, Canberra

'From the day . . . emulate his example.' David Frith, *Australia Versus England: A Pictorial History of Every Test Match Since 1877*, 11th edition, Lothian, South Melbourne, 2002, 7

'Mr Westbrook never . . . both. Cricket won.' Don Bradman, *Farewell to Cricket*, ETT Imprint, Watsons Bay, 1997, 11; first published by Hodder & Stoughton, 1950

They were surprised . . . an astute businessman. A.J. Bell quoted in A.L. Shillinglaw, *Bradman Revisited: The Legacy of Sir Donald Bradman*, The Parrs Wood Press, Manchester, 2003, 60

Bowling to Bradman . . . his temerity merited. *ibid.*

'ordinary, small man in a grey suit'. Graham Perkin, 'Bradman Has Retired, But His Memory Lingers', *Age*, 9/12/59

More than a . . . bowl to him. Michael Parkinson cited in Shillinglaw, *op. cit.*, 159–160

'His greatest critics . . .' . . . Loxton has observed. Sam Loxton, 'My Mate George' in M. Coward (coordinator), *Sir Donald Bradman AC*, Ironbark Legends series, Pan Macmillan Australia, Sydney, 1998, 49

Cricket buff and . . . in their favour. Rodney Cavalier, 'Exploring Frontiers' in *ibid.*, 22

'His lauding of . . .' . . . Hutchins points out. Brett Hutchins, *Don Bradman: Challenging the Myth*, Cambridge University Press, Port Melbourne, 2002, 117

As one of . . . a young cadet. David Bowman letter to Rhyll Rivett, 7/12/96

Murdoch biographer William . . . considered a 'wilderness'. William Shawcross, *Rupert Murdoch: Ringmaster of the Information Circus*, Chatto & Windus, London, 1992, 83

'While taking dictation . . . "for their daughters"!!!' Joy R. Saunders letter to Rhyll Rivett, 14/7/97

'Being a Murdoch man did one no good after Sir Keith died.' Keith Dunstan letter to Rhyll Rivett, 29/1/96

Like the Bradman . . . Library's Rivett papers. Rupert Murdoch letter to Rhyll Rivett, 3/5/96

After 'much long . . .' . . . of the *News*. Rupert Murdoch letter to Rohan Rivett, 5/7/60 in the Rivett Papers, MS 8049, National Library of Australia, Canberra

Dame Elisabeth Murdoch . . . over the move. Elisabeth Murdoch letter to Rohan Rivett, undated, in the Rivett Papers, *ibid.*

During World War . . . Malaya Broadcasting Corporation. K.S. Inglis, 'Rivett, Rohan Deakin' in John Ritchie and Diane Langmore (eds), *Australian Dictionary of Biography*, 1940–1980, vol. 16, MUP, Carlton, 2002, 99–100

Rohan Rivett, *Behind Bamboo: an Inside Story of the Japanese Prison Camps*, Angus & Robertson, London, 1950

Rivett was 'Brainy . . . a One-Off' Delme Forbes letter to Rhyll Rivett, 25/4/96

For forty years . . . in girls' schools. Nancy Rivett, 'The Inspiration Behind the Eleanor and David Rivett Library', unpublished, in the possession of Rhyll Rivett, July 1996

In his unpublished . . . to the *News*. Murdoch letter to Rivett, *op. cit.*

'Probably Mr. Bevan . . . had been alive.' John Miles letter to Rhyll Rivett, 19/4/96

Journalist Keith Dunstan . . . confidence-building style. Dunstan letter to Rivett, *op. cit.*

Rupert 'must learn . . . trouble and study . . .' Shawcross, *op. cit.*, 73

'. . . I don't feel . . . admiration for Nan'. Murray James letter to Rhyll Rivett, 6/5/96

News journalist John . . . a Rohan Rivett. Miles letter to Rivett, *op. cit.*

Rita Dunstan wrote . . . of poor pensioners. Rita Dunstan letter to Rhyll Rivett, 17/2/96

'Often at social . . . for the fund'. Rita Dunstan letter to Rhyll Rivett, 14/3/96

Journalism was a . . . charismatic editor's views. Bowman letter to Rivett, *op. cit.*

The next letter . . . marginally, less formal. MS 8049/2/B2, 25/6/53

'Rohan Rivett Esq. . . . Yours sincerely, Don'. MS 8049/2/B6, 8/7/53

'Warmest regards . . .' MS 8049/2/B7, 20/7/53

'All your investigation . . . No.1 authority thereon'. MS 8049/2/B103

'We are coming . . . no matter what'. MS 8049/2/B12, 9/7/62

The main example . . . were at odds. MS 8049/2/B168, 13/6/75

'Girth is increasing – wisdom doubtful'. MS 8049/2/B8

Chapter 2

'Cricket will ebb . . . our pleasant surprises . . .'. MS 8049/2/B39

The 1953 Lord's . . . to play overall. MS 8049/2/B5, 2/7/53

In contrast the . . . was another draw. MS 8049/2/B7, 20/7/53

Cricket historian Chris . . . Headingley press box. Chris Harte with Bernard Whimpress, *The Penguin History of Australian Cricket*, revised edition, Viking, Camberwell, 2003, 430; first published by Andre Deutsch, London, 1993

England won by . . . for sixty-three years. Frith, *op. cit.*, 190

Pakistan had announced . . . in April 1962. MS 8049/2/B9, 26/4/62

The MCC had . . . the two countries. MS 8049/2/B10, Easter Sunday 1962

'We saw a . . . much at all.' MS 8049/2/B12, 9/7/62

There was no . . . the following year. Fred Trueman cited in Simon Rae, *It's Not Cricket: Cheating, Gamesmanship and the Myth of Fair Play*, Faber & Faber, London, 2002

In early 1964 . . . accompanied the praise. MS 8049/2/B20, 18/2/64

'When Australia was . . . the Sydney Hill.' Harte, *op. cit.*, 485

At one point . . . had just received. MS 8049/2/B27

As the 1964 . . . to the broadcasts. MS 8049/2/B29

'Oh I forgot . . . crossed for Lords.' MS 8049/2/B30

The match led . . . themselves required redraining. Jonathan Rice, *One Hundred Lord's Tests: A Celebration of the Home of Cricket*, Methuen, London, 2001, 99

More thoughts on . . . Bradman thanked him. MS 8049/2/B35, 25/9/64

Bradman was baching . . . and feeling old. MS 8049/2/B36

Simpson scored 311 . . . fifty-five years earlier. Frith, *op. cit.*, 262

Further, he blamed . . . England and Australia. MS 8049/2/B37

Bradman replied, at . . . had stirred 'misgivings'. MS 8049/2/B39

'Taking all things . . . for either side.' MS 8049/2/B44, 1/3/65

In the Second . . . on Australia's fightback. MS 8049/2/B46, 30/3/65

'Ted lapped that . . . be a god.' MS 8049/2/B49

'[As] always, there . . . Bradman is inestimable.' Harte, *op. cit.*, 502–3

There were so . . . and South Africa. MS 8049/2/B61, 22/10/65

In late 1965 . . . base in Australia. MS 8049/2/B73, 25/11/65

'It may be . . . and the schools.' MS 8049/2/B74, 25/11/65

Bradman replied at . . . to discussing it. MS 8049/2/B81, 2/12/65

Six weeks later . . . hold of Rivett. MS 8049/2/B82, 17/1/66

'As usual I . . . all the same.' MS 8049/2/B94, 30/11/66

'And if I . . . direction of R.M.' MS 8049/2/B96

In June Bradman . . . 'Cricketer of the Year'. MS 8049/2/B104, 19/6/67

On top of . . . to turn sixty. MS 8049/2/B102

However, former Test . . . should go on. MS 8049/2/B107

His view that . . . in August 1968. MS 8049/2/B120, 7/8/68

In the Fourth . . . unleashing the ball. Frith, *op. cit.*, 244

At the same . . . simply not right. MS 8049/2/B120, 7/8/68

It upset Bradman . . . whatever actually transpired. MS 8049/2/B122, 31/8/68

'Is Don Bradman Out?' *Age* editorial, 31/8/68

'Like you I . . . on the game'. MS 8049/2/B125, 7/10/68

'The next meeting . . . sponsored games?' Harte, *op. cit.*, 515

In November 1968 . . . recent Shield game. MS 8049/2/B126, 22/11/68

In March 1969 . . . the editorial process. MS 8049/2/B128, 3/3/69

Bradman replied quickly . . . '. . . his bloody cheek . . .' MS 8049/2/B127, 7/3/69

Bradman's reply implies . . . scene in India. MS 8049/2/B131

In the First . . . staying being invaded. Harte, *op. cit.*, 521–2

Would Rivett like . . . in a melee? MS 8049/2/B131

'Negro barrackers were . . . it's your show'. Ray Robinson, *On Top Down Under*, 2nd edition, Cassell Australia, North Ryde, 1981, 134 and picture between 142–3; first published 1975

'Richardson went to . . . his touring colleagues.' Harte, *op. cit.*, 360

'He took me . . . be your cousins'.' *ibid.*, 521

'Despite his faults . . . so many respects,' MS 8049/2/B132, 13/11/69

'We had them . . . brains as a hen.' MS 8049/2/B133, 25/11/69

He believed British . . . with South Africa. MS 8049/2/B135

Rivett might not . . . it due weight. MS 8049/2/B136, 13/7/70

The Board wishes . . . about this end. Harte, *op. cit.*, 533

a 'rainbow' side. *Sir Donald Bradman AC, op. cit.*, 103

In September, as . . . be in order. MS 8049/2/B146, 19/9/71

Bradman thanked him . . . in the aftermath. MS 8049/2/B147, 24/9/71

In mid-1972 the . . . the two men. MS 8049/2/B152, 7/7/72

'Massie's Match'. Rice, *op. cit.*, 120–1

Bradman told Rivett . . . performed any better? MS 8049/2/B152, 7/7/72

Jack Fingleton wrote . . . him from Melbourne. MS 8049/2/B154, 12/2/73

That was what . . . and returned it. MS 8049/2/B155, February 1973

A great batsman . . . *Sydney Morning Herald*. Robinson, *op. cit.*, 141

'Test all-rounder . . . in their writings'. *Sir Donald Bradman AC, op. cit.*, 49

Robinson, the cricket . . . he was not' Robinson, *op. cit.*, 141

Bradman wrote to . . . envy and ego. MS 8049/2/B155

When this letter first came to light Christine Wallace, *Australian* 28/2/04

the Fingleton estate . . . in the report. Malcolm A.Gemmell, 'Bradman's Bodyline Leak', *Australian* 6/3/04

Cricket writer David . . . them in Adelaide. David Frith, *Bodyline Autopsy: The Full Story of the Most Sensational Test Cricket Series: Australia v England 1932–33*, ABC Books, Sydney, 2002, 81–2

'Bradman said to . . . take Allen's bowling.' *ibid.*, 83

'This conviction, although . . . summer of 1930,' Christopher Douglas, *Douglas Jardine: Spartan Cricketer*, Methuen, London, 2003, 124; first published George Allen & Unwin, London, 1984

Fingleton was dropped . . . more cautious performances. Jack Pollard, *Australian Cricket: The Game and the Players*, Hodder & Stoughton, Sydney, 1982, 416

journalist and author . . . club's Trumper Park. *ibid.*, 415–6

'Bradman said it . . . or another, were.' Douglas, *op. cit.*, 140

Fingleton was out . . . out quickly: payback. *ibid.*, 141–2

corroboration for Fingleton's claim. Frith, *Bodyline, op. cit.*, 192–3

whoever was responsible, the leak in fact served cricket well. *ibid.*, 192

After news of . . . here and abroad. Gemmell, *op. cit.*

'48 years on and still dreaming about it'. Douglas, *op. cit.*, 142

Rivett's missive in February 1973. MS 8049/2/B155, February 1973

Christopher Douglas describes . . . of the series. Douglas, *op. cit.*, 142–4

Bradman outlined how . . . with bodyline bowling. Donald Bradman, *Farewell to Cricket, op. cit.*

From that distance . . . quite top level. MS 8049/2/B155

In March 1973 . . . the health front. MS 8049/2/B157, 18/3/73

Massie had suddenly . . . serious back injury. Pollard, *op. cit.*, 1085

A few months . . . effective from September. MS 8049/2/B159, 6/7/73

A plethora of . . . associations that year. Harte, *op. cit.*, 542

Ian Chappell locates . . . in the 1970s. Ian Chappell, *Chappelli: The Cutting Edge*, Swan, Nedland, 1992, 42–52

'Ian, a rebel . . . of later years.' Harte, *op. cit.*, 486

In October 1976 . . . for a function. MS 8049/2/B171, 3/10/76

'It was an . . . approach to life'. MS 8049/2/B172, 3/10/76

But not before . . . exchange on selection. MS 8049/2/B186

Neither man knew . . . such things were. MS 8049/2/B187, 18/3/1977

Rivett wrote, in . . . of traditional cricket. MS 8049/2/B190

Arguably, the jury . . . of the game.' MS 8049/2/B39

CHAPTER 3

'Should I sell News yet?' MS 8049/2/B18, 21/8/63

Australian resource stock . . . the Rivett Papers. MS 8049/2/B9, 26/4/62

Easter 1962 saw . . . not very active. MS 8049/2/B10, Easter Sunday 1962

In June 1962 . . . in one sentence. MS 8049/2/B11, 25/6/62

Writing from Montreaux . . . of forty-two stocks. MS 8049/2/B12, 9/7/62

'My main comment . . . it was mine.' MS 8049/2/B13, 18/7/62

Rivett wrote to Bradman in May about purchasing shares. This letter is not in the Rivett Papers but is referred to by Bradman in MS 8049/2/B14, 20/5/63

'Oh – just saw . . . up. Don't know.' MS 8049/2/B14, 20/5/63

'You will [thus] . . . a better bargain.' *ibid.*

Bradman's next letter . . . wrong-headedly stubborn behaviour. MS 8049/2/B15, 31/5/63

But the next . . . friendly personal terms. MS 8049/2/B17, 30/7/63

It had already . . . those missives on. MS 8049/2/B18, 21/8/63

A middle course . . . investment advice seriously. MS 8049/2/B16, 27/8/63

But things were . . . investment dialogue resumed. MS 8049/2/B21, 10/3/64

By May health . . . the investment chat. MS 8049/2/B24, 6/5/64

Bradman subsequently stirred . . . media stock calls. MS 8049/2/B27

Wage increases not . . . worry to Bradman. MS 8049/2/B30

In September 1964 . . . in some detail MS 8049/2/B31–34, 19/9/64

a follow-up on Rivett's subsequent comments MS 8049/2/B25, 25/9/64

Bradman told Rivett . . .'. . . their big problem'. MS 8049/2/B33, 19/9/64

Conversely, he favoured . . . would do better. MS 8049/2/B35, 25/9/64

The uranium stock . . .'. . . mystery' to him. MS 8049/2/B33, 19/9/64

The market was . . . for a year. MS 8049/2/B36

Bradman remained sceptical' MS 8049/2/B38

In the run-up . . . potential share trades. MS 8049/2/B39

And still the . . . continued to fascinate. MS 8049/2/B42

One came in . . . Pulp and APM. MS 8049/2/B43, 22/1/65

March 1965 saw . . . like Yarra Falls. MS 8049/2/B44, 1/3/65

The 1965 UK . . . on the rise. MS 8049/2/B48, 7/4/65

Renison, which Rivett . . . a possible exception. MS 8049/2/B49

Subsequently he cooled . . . was too speculative. MS 8049/2/B52

Overall Bradman's view of the market remained sober. MS 8049/2/B51

As 1965 continued . . . to be profitable. MS 8049/2/B54, 16/8/65

In September 1965 . . . company's then state. MS 8049/2/B56

Rivett wrote straight . . . News' annual result. MS 8049/2/B57, 20/9/65

'Of one thing . . . no influence whatever'. MS 8049/2/B58, 27/9/65

But against the . . . time, Bradman argued. MS 8049/2/B59, 27/9/65

A takeover had . . . Tom Playford – intervened. MS 8049/2/B60, 27/9/65

In October 1965 . . . first wife, Prudence. MS 8049/2/B62, 27/10/65

With exceptions, Bradman remained somewhat bearish. MS 8049/2/B87

The older he . . . into the future. MS 8049/2/B88, 22/8/66

Bradman again provided . . . eight separate stocks. MS 8049/2/B89

In September 1966 . . . of the market. MS 8049/2/B92, 14/9/66

But Bradman had . . . to the money. MS 8049/2/B93, 6/11/66

In November 1966 . . . Herald and Ansett. MS 8049/2/B94, 30/11/66

April 1967 saw . . . an investment matter. MS 8049/2/B97, 24/4/67

'Thank goodness clients . . . advice on investments'. MS 8049/2/B99

Bradman steered Rivett . . . in Ansett debentures. MS 8049/2/B106, 19/6/67

'In any case . . . up to $3?' MS 8049/2/B101, July 1967

Around this time . . . make investment decisions. MS 8049/2/B107

In August 1967 . . . Rivett thought highly. MS 8049/2/B108, 11/8/67

In August 1967 . . . of meat stocks. MS 8049/2/B110, 14/8/67

The next day . . . number of stocks. MS 8049/2/B111, 15/8/67

Bradman revisited the issue in September. MS 8049/2/B113, 23/9/67

in October renewed . . . Rivett's risk orientation. MS 8049/2/B114, 5/10/67

A visit to . . . he added oil. MS 8049/2/B115, 20/10/67

The following year . . . Australia's declining prospects. MS 8049/2/B119

The reverberations of . . . dialogue with Rivett. MS 8049/2/B122, 31/8/68

'The market gave . . . mining deserved it'. MS 8049/2/B125, 7/10/68

He believed much . . . by inflationary fears. MS 8049/2/B119

'Our markets are . . .' . . . interest rates abroad' MS 8049/2/B8

'I must be . . . parcel of News'. MS 8049/2/B126, 22/11/68

As for the . . .' . . . away and forget'. MS 8049/2/B130, 8/8/69

October 1969 saw . . . at that time. MS 8049/2/B131

'For some time . . . the share market'. MS 8049/2/B132, 13/11/69

Another fortnight hence . . . demented to Bradman. MS 8049/2/B133, 25/11/69

South Australia's attractions . . . in Bradman's view. MS 8049/2/B135

But even as . . . the previous week. MS 8049/2/B149, 13/3/72

In late 1973 . . . the Whitlam administration. MS 8049/2/B162, 25/10/73

On the verge . . . extended trip abroad. MS 8049/2/B165

'property is the best in an inflationary era'. MS 8049/2/B178, 15/11/76

Bradman saw continuing . . . the Whitlam period. MS 8049/2/B179, 15/11/76

E&OE, Errors and omissions excepted

A few weeks . . . his own portfolio. MS 8049/2/B192a, 19/9/77

CHAPTER 4

'. . . my political philosophy . . . I believe in.' MS8049/2/B166, 9/6/75

Long-serving Australian . . . sobriquet of 'Ming' MS 8049/2/B61, 22/10/65

'Why – The News . . . Brazil or somewhere.' MS 8049/2/B13, 18/7/62

'You must be . . . in our lifetime.' MS 8049/2/B11, 25/6/62

'The political background . . . and wreck him'. MS 8049/2/B17, 30/7/63

my suspicious nature . . . is 'well meaning'. MS 8049/2/B27

One example was . . . international economic developments. MS 8049/2/B27

'As for politics . . . are we heading?' MS 8049/2/B29

While the outlook . . . attend testimonial dinners. MS 8049/2/B46, 30/3/65

The 1965 UK . . . imposed here eventually. MS 8049/2/B48, 7/4/65

'Your views on . . . the cricket tour'. MS 8049/2/B61

'Did Ming entertain you?' MS 8049/2/B61, 22/10/65

'The world is . . . than I do . . .' MS 8049/2/B63, 12/11/65

One certainty, Bradman . . . in the future. MS 8049/2/B87

'The modern tendency . . . before the horse'. MS 8049/2/B88, 22/8/66

In September 1966 . . . a recent letter. MS 8049/2/B92, 14/9/66

In late 1966 . . . on development there. MS 8049/2/B93, 6/11/66

November brought not . . . in one paragraph. MS 8049/2/B94, 30/11/66

'I am a . . . left or right'. MS 8049/2/B95, December 1966

The likelihood of . . . raised by Rivett. MS 8049/2/B104, 19/6/67

Bradman believed that . . . constrain the media. MS 8049/2/B110, 14/8/67

Dunstan and his . . . premier, Steele Hall. MS 8049/2/B119

In October 1968 . . . on the game. MS 8049/2/B125, 7/10/68

Exchange rates worldwide . . . of 'government mismanagement'. MS 8049/2/B126, 22/11/68

John Gorton's narrow . . . as, essentially, slackers. MS 8049/2/B131

'I hate politicians . . . to their convictions'. MS 8049/2/B135

In September 1971 . . . his recent letter. MS 8049/2/B147, 24/9/71

Four months after . . . to worsen rapidly. MS 8049/2/B157, 18/3/73

'Whitlam permitting', Bradman . . . at the time. MS 8049/2/B159, 6/7/73

A few months . . . '. . . Crean & Co'. MS 8049/2/B160, 16/9/73

'All I know . . . all be broke . . .'. MS 8049/2/B161, 16/10/73

'I doubt if . . . have done already.' MS 8049/2/B162, 25/10/73

Rivett wrote in . . . hardly been harmonious. MS 8049/2/B166, 9/6/75

Bradman was stunned . . . a company director. MS 8049/2/B164, 9/6/75

Trade Practices Act 1974

Bradman was dismissive . . . '. . . system' in Australia. MS 8049/2/B166, 9/6/75

Former Treasury economist . . . of the problem. Don Russell, 'The Role of Executive Government in Australia', Department of the Senate Occasional Lecture Series, Parliament House, Canberra, 25 October 2002

Kipling's two imposters. 'If you can meet with triumph and disaster/ And treat those two imposters just the same', from *If* by Rudyard Kipling

'I think in . . . be too long'. MS 8049/2/B167, 9/6/75

As he had . . . the national interest. MS 8049/2/B170

'That is why . . . by his performance . . .' MS 8049/2/B170a

Bradman told Rivett . . . 'frustrating and worrying'. MS 8049/2/B171, 3/10/76

'Society doesn't seem . . . or a Ford'. MS 8049/2/B172

It concerned the . . . the mid-1970s on. MS 8049/2/B177

The doubts Rivett . . . Melbourne and Sydney. MS 8049/2/B176a, 27/10/76

CHAPTER 5

'. . . the press, with . . . which are good.' MS 8049/2/B120, 7/8/68

Bradman's engagement by . . . in the series. MS 8049/2/Bradman 1, 5/5/53

The very next . . . the Lord's Test. MS 8049/2/B2, 25/6/53

'I shall do my best to help you out.' *ibid.*

'Rest assured I . . . won't manufacture criticism'. MS 8049/2/B3, 25/6/53

'I don't know . . . of avoiding newspapermen.' MS 8049/2/B4, 25/6/53

He warned Rivett . . . were not common. MS 8049/2/B5, 2/7/53

In a letter . . . arriving fast enough. MS 8049/2/B6, 8/7/53

Bradman's warning about . . . Year English summer. MS 8049/2/B7, 20/7/53

He had earlier . . . possibility with Rivett. MS 8049/2/B5, 2/7/53

Rivett must have . . . something badly wrong. MS 8049/2/B7, 20/7/53

In April 1962 . . . had come across. MS 8049/2/B9, 26/4/62

Rivett's belated response . . .'. . . prostitutes' of journalism. MS 8049/2/B12, 9/7/62

Rivett's call was . . . 'outburst' regarding Lippman. MS 8049/2/B13, 18/7/62

In the mid-1960s . . . about the deal. MS 8049/2/B25

Negative, low grade . . . feeding the problem. MS 8049/2/B39

Rivett's attempt to . . . with the media. MS 8049/2/B120, 7/8/68

So much in . . . Rivett in 1971. MS 8049/2/B147, 24/9/71

News coverage the . . . by the media. MS 8049/2/B149, 13/3/72

'Yes, I'm still bread & jam to the press . . .'. MS 8049/2/B161, 16/10/73

In April 1974 . . . for New Zealand. MS 8049/2/B163

Bradman was bemused . . . when they wanted. MS 8049/2/B164, 9/6/75

Bradman regrettably declined . . . up public speaking. MS 8049/2/B165, 9/6/75

'The problem is . . . in the world.' MS 8049/2/B172, 3/10/76

CHAPTER 6

'Life seems to . . . and imagining things.' MS 8049/2/B58, 27/9/65

'Love from all . . . As ever, mate . . .' MS 8049/2/B12, 9/7/62

The first extensive . . . for the *News*. MS 8049/2/B2, 25/6/53

But at the . . . so very quickly. MS 8049/2/B3–4, 25/6/53

One of the . . . Melbourne's Hotel Windsor. MS 8049/2/B83

In April 1962 . . . or the weather. MS 8049/2/B9, 26/4/62

The weather had . . . on its way. MS 8049/2/B10, Easter Sunday 1962

Bradman apologised that . . . Rivett's interesting missives. MS 8049/2/B11, 25/6/62

In a long . . . John Bradman's knee. MS 8049/2/B12, 9/7/62

A letter the . . . beauty of France. MS 8049/2/B14, 20/5/63

Bradman was so . . . pressure of time. MS 8049/2/B

'Fancy having to . . . if I fail.' MS 8049/2/B16, 27/8/63

The death of . . . such a time. MS 8049/2/B20, 18/2/64

Rivett offered counsel . . . still without result. MS 8049/2/B22, 27/2/64

Bradman told Rivett . . . their Kensington home. MS 8049/2/B21, 10/3/64

The impending 1964 Ashes series lifted spirits all round. MS 8049/2/B23, 20/4/64

'I, too, had a . . . I was wrong.' MS 8049/2/B24, 6/5/64

As the 1960s . . . it had previously. MS 8049/2/B27

But an air . . . dot the correspondence. MS 8049/2/B29

One letter reeled . . . friends and associates. MS 8049/2/B30

The health woes . . . wrote to Rivett. MS 8049/2/B31, 19/9/64

Mercifully, Rivett's reply was typed. MS 8049/2/B35, 25/9/64

In fact, Bradman was in a weakened state. MS 8049/2/B36

One four page . . .'. . . must keep trying'. MS 8049/2/B39

'I've never been . . . like this before'. MS 8049/2/B42

There was light . . . 'quite a handful'. MS 8049/2/B43

In March Bradman . . . in Frankston, Victoria. MS 8049/2/B44, 1/3/65

They were feeling . . . giving her trouble. MS 8049/2/B46, 30/3/65

A week later . . . was no better. MS 8049/2/B47, 6/4/65

'His outlook couldn't . . . a real problem.' MS 8049/2/B48, 7/4/65

During Rivett's trip . . . on his return. MS 8049/2/B50, 2/7/65

This triggered a round of joshing between the two. MS 8049/2/B54, 16/8/65

'But that is . . . avoid our responsibilities'. MS 8049/2/B55

Bradman spent a . . . drenched with rain. MS 8049/2/B56

Jessie's wrist was . . . late September 1965. MS 8049/2/B57, 20/9/65

In October 1965 . . . might be imminent. MS 8049/2/B61, 22/10/65

'It was like . . . point of view.' MS 8049/2/B63, 12/11/65

During the Sydney . . . to Rivett afterwards. MS 8049/2/B82, 17/1/66

A major development . . . studies in Adelaide. MS 8049/2/B84, 1/4/66

After the Frankston . . . Kensington at all. MS 8049/2/B85

John Bradman's moodiness . . . the tender subject. MS 8049/2/B87

It was bad . . . friend, Barby Williss. MS 8049/2/B88, 22/8/66

In the meantime . . . Richardson's cricketing career. MS 8049/2/B87

'Firstly dealing with Nan's P.S.'. MS 8049/2/B88, 22/8/66

As 1966 drew . . . them get together. MS 8049/2/B93, 6/11/66

As often seemed . . . as Bradman's guest. MS 8049/2/B94, 30/11/66

The Rivetts planned a mid-year break in Port Willunga. MS 8049/2/B97, 24/4/67

In the return . . . the Frankston stay. MS 8049/2/B98, 28/4/67

'Great excitement on her part – tremendous apprehension on mine'. MS 8049/2/B100

June 1967 saw . . . Adelaide's alleged big-timers. MS 8049/2/B104, 19/6/67

In the meantime . . . at Rivett's request. MS 8049/2/B110, 14/8/67

In August 1967 . . . about Rivett's portfolio. MS 8049/2/B111, 15/8/67

Bradman replied that . . . to do so. MS 8049/2/B113, 23/9/67

Bradman replied that . . . out of touch. MS 8049/2/B114, 5/10/67

In October 1967 . . . 're-rating' Melbourne's elite. MS 8049/2/B115

While he never . . . everyone, like bills. MS 8049/2/B102

But Bradman's three . . . a fortnight's time. MS 8049/2/B103

Family worries were always uppermost in Bradman's mind. MS 8049/2/B107

The Bradmans had . . . taken seriously ill. MS 8049/2/B118, 13/12/67

A few months later, things had steadied. MS 8049/2/B119

On 31 August . . .'. . . the letters etc'. MS 8049/2/B122, 31/8/68

'The News Racing . . .' . . . paper's front page. MS 8049/2/B124

In October 1968 . . . a little easier. MS 8049/2/B125, 7/10/68

The following month . . . doctors for x-rays. MS 8049/2/B126, 22/11/68

By early 1969 . . . the family's concerns. MS 8049/2/B127, 7/3/69

The following month . . . home in Melbourne. MS 8049/2/B129, 18/4/69

There was no . . . over the summer. MS 8049/2/B130, 8/8/69

Rohan Rivett, *David Rivett: Fighter for Australian Science*, R.D. Rivett, Camberwell, 1972

Bradman pushed him on. MS8049/2/B130

The buoyancy did . . . 'in many directions'. MS 8049/2/B131

Towards the end . . . on his children. MS 8049/2/B133, 25/11/69

On Christmas Eve . . . the New Year. MS 8049/2/B134, 24/12/69

Leslie Haylen, *Twenty Years' Hard Labor*, Macmillan, South Melbourne, 1969

Robert Menzies, *Afternoon Light, Some Memories of Men and Events*, Penguin, Ringwood, 1969; first published Cassell Australia, 1967

A bad back . . . resume playing golf. MS 8049/2/B135

But the next . . . on beef cattle. MS 8049/2/B139, 3/8/70

'That's the end'. MS 8049/2/B143, 18/12/70

At Rohan's request . . . was a director. MS 8049/2/B144, 25/2/71

September 1971 saw . . . Rohan and Nan. MS 8049/2/B146, 19/9/71

In the winter . . . a punishing schedule. MS 8049/2/B147, 24/9/71

On 13 March . . . they had unfolded. MS 8049/2/B149, 13/3/72

Bradman's reply was . . . his earlier letter. MS 8049/2/B150, 30/3/72

Rivett quickly replied . . . John's actions. MS 8049/2/B151, 7/4/72

By mid-winter the . . . correspondence with Rivett. MS 8049/2/B152, 7/7/72

But Bradman added a quick rider. MS 8049/2/B153, 7/7/72

'The wine was . . . we were grateful.' MS 8049/2/B155, February 1973

He replied that . . . the reflected glory. MS 8049/2/B156, 18/3/73

Jessie's blood condition . . . Bradman told Rivett. MS 8049/2/B157, 18/3/73

When Rivett wrote . . . could be squeezed. MS 8049/2/B158, 26/8/73

In July he . . . effective from September. MS 8049/2/159, 6/7/73

By spring Bradman . . .'. . . chat at leisure'. MS 8049/2/B160, 16/9/73

But a month . . . couples in December. MS 8049/2/B161, 16/10/73

In April 1974 . . . prime winemaking region. MS 8049/2/B163, 23/4/74

The otherwise enjoyable . . . up public speaking. MS 8049/2/B165, 9/6/75

Bradman sympathised but . . . little further north. MS 8049/2/B165, 9/6/75

The Rivetts were . . . make it worthwhile. MS 8049/2/B166, 9/6/75

The juxtaposition led . . . optimism and pessimism. MS 8049/2/B167, 9/6/75

'your public utterances . . . your private behaviour'. MS 8049/2/B166, 9/6/75

Rivett's response – three . . . the Middle East. MS 8049/2/B168, 13/6/75

Just because one . . . on frivolous self-indulgence. MS 8049/2/B168a, 13/6/75

Nan had developed . . . Lebanon and Syria. MS 8049/2/B169, 13/6/75

By summer Bradman . . . January of 1976. MS 8049/2/B170

The correspondence slowed . . . blamed the fates. MS 8049/2/B171, 3/10/76

Were Rohan and . . . the US yet? MS 8049/2/B172, 3/10/76

He dashed off . . .'. . . bit over first'. MS 8049/2/B186

It was in . . . for 17 October. MS 8049/2/B187, 18/3/77

Bradman wrote to . . . a fortnight earlier. MS 8049/2/B188, 25/4/77

'But to see . . . is terribly sad.' MS 8049/2/B190

Despite the risks . . . triple bypass surgery. MS 8049/2/B191

'In the 35 . . . let anyone down.' MS 8049/2/B192, 19/9/77

Against this backdrop . . . had suddenly died. MS 8049/2/B193

CHAPTER 7

'. . . my friends are . . . any other way.' MS 8049/2/B167, 9/6/75

'He meant so . . . to harm him.' Frith, *Bodyline*, *op. cit.*, 78

After some years using the surname 'Bradsen' John Bradman resumed use of his family surname.

'japemanship to a heartless extreme unlikely to be forgotten.' Robinson, *op. cit.*, 139–40

Select Bibliography

Bradman, D., *Farewell to Cricket*, ETT Imprint, Watsons Bay, 1997, first published Hodder & Stoughton, 1950

Bradman, D., letters to Rohan Rivett, Rivett Papers, MS 8049, National Library of Australia, Canberra

Chappell, I., *Chappelli: The Cutting Edge*, Swan, Nedlands, 1992

Coward, M. (coordinator), *Sir Donald Bradman AC*, Ironbark Legends series, Pan Macmillan Australia, Sydney 1998

Douglas, C., *Douglas Jardine, Spartan Cricketer*, Methuen, London, 2003, first published George Allen & Unwin, London, 1984

Frith, D., *Australia Versus England: A Pictorial History of Every Test Match Since 1877*, 11th edition, Lothian, South Melbourne, 2002

Frith, D., *Bodyline Autopsy: The Full Story of the Most Sensational Test Cricket Series: Australia v England 1932–33*, ABC Books, Sydney, 2002

Harte, C. with Whimpress, B., *The Penguin History of Australian Cricket*, revised edition, Viking, Camberwell, 2003, first published Andre Deutsch, London, 1993

Hutchins, B., *Don Bradman: Challenging the Myth*, Cambridge University Press, Port Melbourne, 2002

Inglis, K.S., 'Rivett, Rohan Deakin' in *Australian Dictionary of Biography*, 1940–1980, v. 16, Melbourne University Press, Carlton, 2002

Pollard, J., *Australian Cricket: The Game and the Players*, Hodder & Staughton, Sydney, 1982

Rae, S., *It's Not Cricket: Cheating, Gamesmanship and the Myth of Fair Play*, Faber & Faber, London, 2002

Rice, J., *One Hundred Lord's Tests: A Celebration of the Home of Cricket*, Methuen, London, 2001

Rivett, N., 'The Inspiration Behind the Eleanor and David Rivett Library', unpublished, July 1996

Rivett, R., letters to Donald Bradman, Rivett Papers, MS 8049, National Library of Australia, Canberra

Rivett, R., *Behind Bamboo: An Inside Story of the Japanese Prison Camps*, Angus & Robertson, London, 1950

Robinson, R., *On Top Down Under*, 2nd edition, Cassell Australia, North Ryde, 1981

Shawcross, W., *Rupert Murdoch: Ringmaster of the Information Circus*, Chatto & Windus, London, 1992

Shillinglaw, A.L., *Bradman Revisited: The Legacy of Sir Donald Bradman*, The Parrs Wood Press, Manchester, 2003

Acknowledgements

Thanks to the National Library of Australia especially Director-General Jan Fullerton, Margy Burn, Graeme Powell, Yvonne Kennedy and the excellent staff of the Manuscripts Reading Room.

Thanks also to Chris Mitchell and Bruce Guthrie at the *Australian*; Lyn Tranter of Australian Literary Management; Sue Hines and Clare Emery at Allen & Unwin; editor Jo Jarrah and designer Phil Campbell; and Shannon Platt, Susan Lawry and Caroline Atkins at Phillips Fox.

Thanks to Christie Costello, Laura Grande, Monica Thompson and Julia Markowski for cover consultations and coffee.

Special thanks to Nancy Rivett and Rhyll Rivett for their time and generous guidance.

Christine Wallace
Canberra 2004

Photographic Credits

FRONTISPIECE
Courtesy of Getty Images

CHAPTER OPENINGS
Chapter 1: Courtesy of Getty Images
Chapter 2: Courtesy of the Adelaide *Advertiser*
Chapter 3: Copyright and courtesy of John Fairfax Limited
Chapter 4: Copyright the Adelaide *Advertiser*, courtesy of the State Library of South Australia (PRG682_13_90.jpg)
Chapters 5, 6 & 7: Courtesy of the Adelaide *Advertiser*

ILLUSTRATED SECTIONS
Illustrated Section 1
Page 1: Courtesy of the Adelaide *Advertiser*
Page 2: From the Rivett Papers, courtesy of the National Library of Australia
Page 3: Courtesy of the Adelaide *Advertiser*
Page 4: Courtesy of Getty Images
Pages 5 & 6: Courtesy of the Adelaide *Advertiser*
Pages 7 & 8: From the Rivett Papers, courtesy of the National Library of Australia

Illustrated Section 2
Page 9: From the Rivett Papers, courtesy of the National Library of Australia
Page 10, upper: From the *Argus* collection, courtesy of the State Library of Victoria
Page 10, lower: Courtesy of the Adelaide *Advertiser*
Pages 11, 12 & 13: Copyright and courtesy of the Adelaide *Advertiser*
Page 14: Copyright and courtesy of the National Archives of Australia
Page 15: Courtesy of the Rivett family
Page 16: Copyright and courtesy of the Adelaide *Advertiser*

Index

Page numbers in italics refer to pages in the illustrated sections. Page numbering in the illustrated sections is independent of page numbering in the body text.